For my beloved son-friend

from

Gigi   6/21/98

Psalms
for Praying

Psalms
for Praying

. . . .

AN INVITATION

TO WHOLENESS

Nan C. Merrill

CONTINUUM   •   NEW YORK

1996
The Continuum Publishing Company
370 Lexington Avenue
New York, NY 10017

Printed in the United States of America

Library of Congress Cataloging-in-Publication Data

Merrill, Nan C.
   Psalms for praying : an invitation to wholeness / Nan C. Merrill.
      p.   cm.
   ISBN 0-8264-0930-X (hardcover : alk. paper)
   1. Bible. O.T. Psalms—Prayers. I. Title.
BS1430.5.M47   1996
223'.205209—dc20   96-20363
                                                           CIP

Dedicated to
the indwelling Divine Guest
whose Voice is heard
in the Silence

Preface

*W*ho among us has not yearned TO KNOW the Unknowable? For most, these moments are fleeting glimpses that may last a lifetime; in some, a Fire is kindled and life becomes a quest to live in Holy Surrender; and though fewer in number, saints dwell among us who know the Beloved, who aspire simply to co-create in harmony with the One, who is Love and Light and Power. To cherish the Beloved as you are cherished is to live in a mutual bonding that calls for action.

The Psalms have ever been a response to these deep yearnings: cries of the soul . . . songs of surrender . . . paeans of praise. The Psalms of the Hebrew Scripture often reflect a patriarchal society based on fear and guilt that projects evil and sin onto outer enemies. *Psalms for Praying* reflects the reciprocity of Divine Love that opens the heart to forgiveness, reconciliation, and healing. Affirming the life-giving fruits of love and acknowledging the isolation and loneliness of those separated from Love, may serve to awaken the heart to move toward wholeness and holiness.

Aspiring to live in a spirit of cooperation, co-creation, and companionship with the Beloved, rather than invoking a spirit of competition with God, other individuals and nations—so much a part of the Hebrew Scripture Psalms—seems clearly a more loving movement toward engendering peace, harmony, and healing in our wounded world.

Yet, let it be understood that *Psalms for Praying: An Invitation to Wholeness* is in no way meant to replace the well-loved, still meaningful, and historically important Psalms of the Hebrew Scripture. May it stand as a companion, a dialogue, if you will, of one age speaking with a later age. May it serve as an invitation to listen to the Voice of Silence that speaks within your own soul.

Psalm 1

Blessed are those
    who walk hand in hand
        with goodness,
    who stand beside virtue,
    who sit in the seat of truth;
For their delight is in the Spirit of Love,
    and in Love's heart they dwell
        day and night.
They are like trees planted by
        streams of water,
    that yield fruit in due season,
    and their leaves flourish;
And in all that they do, they give life.
The unloving are not so;
    they are like dandelions which
        the wind blows away.
Turning from the Heart of Love
    they will know suffering and pain.
They will be isolated from wisdom;
    for Love knows the way of truth,
    the way of ignorance will perish.

Psalm 2

Why do nations and people plot against
                    one another,
      setting themselves apart and conspiring
              against the Beloved and those
              who follow Love's way?
They say to themselves, "We are free
              of Love's law;
      humility and service are for others."

The Beloved, who is ever present, can but
              smile at their foolishness,
      knowing that one day, they will
              fall to their knees in regret.
They do not hear the Beloved's firm and
              steadfast voice:
"I have set Love in your hearts,
      my dwelling place."

Let me share the way of Love:
Love calls to us, "You are mine;
      this day I become your Beloved;
          ask of me what you will.
    I give you all nations,
    the whole universe, to care for,
        to be your delight.
    You will shatter fear as an iron rod
        hitting a clay pot."

Listen then, you leaders of nations,
Heed well, O people of the earth.

Serve the Beloved with reverence;
      bow your heads and embrace Love.
Otherwise, ignorance and fear will
        be your companions
      bringing destruction and despair.

Blessed are all who dwell in Love!

Psalm 3

O Beloved, how numerous are my fears!
      They rise up within me whispering
      there is no help for you in Love.

Yet You, O my Beloved, radiate around me,
        my glory,
      lifting my head high.
I cry aloud to You,
      and You answer within my heart.

I lie down and sleep;
      I wake again, for my Beloved
        holds me with strength
        and tenderness.
      I shall withstand all my fears
        as they arise within me.

Rise up, Love!

Set me free, my Beloved!
>for with You in my heart
>my fears will be transformed
>>into Love.

Freedom from fear comes through Love;
May the Beloved's blessing reign within
>all hearts!

Psalm 4

Answer me when I call, O Beloved of my heart!
You enveloped me in Love when I
>was in distress.
Be gracious to me now; hear my prayer.

O friends, how long will my reputation
>suffer shame?
How long will you listen to false words
>and seek what is less than good?

You know that the Beloved dwells with those
>who are filled with love;
>and hears when our hearts cry out.
Though you may feel angry,
>do not give in to fear;

Commune with the Heart of your heart
          as you rest,
     and be in silence.
Make peace with your fears,
          and trust in Love.

There are many who say,
          "Grant us special favors,
               O Mighty One!
          Bestow upon us your grace that
               we may prosper!"
          Love has brought more joy to my heart
               than they have when their banks
                    are filled.
In peace will I spend my days and
          sleep at night;
For You alone, my Beloved,
          take away my fears.

Psalm 5

Give ear to my words, O my Beloved;
          give heed to my groaning.
Listen to the sound of my cry,
          my Love, Heart of my heart,
          for to You do I pray.
O my Beloved, in the morning

You hear my voice;
in the morning I offer myself to You,
and wait for You in silence.
For You are love and You delight
in goodness;
all that is of love walks with You.
The humble stand before You;
You dwell with those who open
their hearts.
You smile on those who speak truth;
tears from your Heart fall on those
separated from You by fear.

Through the abundance of your steadfast love
I shall enter your house;
I shall worship in your holy temple
with reverence for You.

Lead me, O my Beloved, in your mercy
lighten my fears;
make your way straight before me
that I may follow.
For there is no truth in fear;
it leads to downfall;
it opens the door to loneliness;
it speaks not with integrity,
but out of ignorance;
Let this guilt I bear, my Beloved,
be seen in your light;
forgive the many false ways I have,
surround them with your love,
for they keep me separated from You.

Let all who come to Love rejoice,
let them sing for joy!
And protect them, that those

who live in your love may
dance in your light.
For You do bless the peaceful and just,
O my Beloved;
You encircle them with your healing light
and enfold them in love.

Psalm 6

O my Beloved, though I have turned from You,
continue to enfold me with your love;
Be gracious to me, Heart of my heart,
for I am sad and weary.
Surround me with your healing Light,
that my body, mind, and soul might heal.
How long must I wait, O Love?

I open the door of my heart to You,
my Beloved,
Enter in and imbue me with your steadfast Love.
I shall remember You all my days;
I shall sing praises to You throughout the
nights.

I am tired of so many fears;
I cry myself to sleep at night;
grief and feelings of guilt
bedim my eyes with tears;

All my doubts, my fears, are creating walls
        so that I know not love.

Depart from me,
        you enemies of wholeness,
        for the Beloved is aware of my cry;
Love has heard my prayer;
        and hastens to answer my call.
Though my fears are running for cover,
        yet they shall be transformed
            by Love;
All that was in darkness shall come
        into the Light.

Psalm 7

O my Beloved, to You do I draw close;
        when all my inner fears well up,
        enfold me in your strong arms;
        otherwise, like a fiery dragon,
            my fears will consume me and
            I shall live in darkness.

O Love, if I have been unkind,
        unloving, or acted in ignorance,
        if I have been unjust to others
            seeing my own weaknesses in them,

Forgive me, O Gracious One,
  and give me the grace to make amends,
  that we may walk again in harmony.

Arise, O Beloved, in your steadfast love,
  shield me from the demons within;
Stay near me, Heart of my heart, and
  I shall be strong to face
    my fears.
Let all the fragmented parts of my being
    gather around You,
  help me to face them one by one.
Love's healing presence will mend
    all that has been broken,
  and I shall be made whole.

O let the terrible fears that keep me
  from loving come to an end!
Establish integrity within me,
  You who test our minds and hearts;
  You who call us to wisdom and love.

My shield is with Love,
  who dwells within my open heart.
Love is kind and gracious,
  quick to forgive and pleased
    to share
  the great Mystery of life!

If I close my heart to Love,
  the Beloved awaits close by;
Love cultivates the soil of my heart,
  planting seeds in its garden.
Take notice! Even should I wander

far from Love's path,
though I err and walk on roads
of illusion and darkness,
should I act out of fear and
ignorance,
falling into a pit of despair,
Yet will Love remain constant and sure.
I shall dwell with Love in gratitude
and joy;
I shall sing praises to the Beloved,
Heart of my heart!

Psalm 8

O Love, my Beloved,
How powerful is your Name
in all the earth!
You, whose glory is sung in heaven
by the angels and saints,
Who with the innocence and
spontaneity of a child,
Confound those who are mighty
and proud,
You quiet the unloving and fearful.

When I look up at the heavens,
at the work of Love's creation,

at the infinite variety of your Plan;
What is woman that you rejoice in her,
And man that you do delight in him?
You have made us in your image,
You fill us with your Love;
You have made us co-creators of
the earth!
guardians of the planet!
to care for all your creatures,
to tend the land, the sea,
and the air we breathe;
all that You have made,
You have placed in our hands.

O Love, my Beloved,
How powerful is your Name in
all the earth!

Psalm 9

Give thanks to the Beloved
with your whole heart;
tell the story of Love's way;
Be glad and dance with joy;
Sing praises to the Name above
all names,
as illusions are dispelled,

as they fade away before
            Love's face.
For You, O Beloved, are ever-present,
      ready to enter open hearts.

You cry over the nations, seeing
            how they destroy one another;
            chaos and darkness rise up
                  blind to Love's way;
            forgotten is creation's glory,
            false power seeks to destroy
                  The Divine Plan.
Yet Love will abide forever;
You have established yourself
                  in secret places
            seeking out receptive hearts,
            ready to enter and make your
                  dwelling place within.

Love is a stronghold for the oppressed,
            a foundation in difficult times.
And those who know Love's Name
            therein place their trust.
For You, O Beloved, are ever-present
            to those who search for You.

Sing praises to the One, who is Love,
            who dwells in your heart!
Tell everyone of Love's wonder-
                  filled deeds!
For those who know compassion
            will remember those in need.

Be gracious to me, O Beloved!
     Behold what I suffer out of fear,
     O You, who awakened me from
          a living death,
     that I might tell of your glory,
     that from the depths of my being,
I may rejoice and give thanks for
          your faithful love.

The nations are sinking into a pit
          of their own making;
     into the web which they are weaving,
          will they be caught.
Love will make Itself known;
With a strength stronger than
          ten thousand armies!
The unloving will have to face
          themselves,
     all nations that depart from Love.
For the oppressed will be released,
And the hope of the poor will
          be realized.

Arise, O Love! Have your way with us;
     let the nations bow before You
          and ask forgiveness!
Let your healing Light stream forth,
          O Love,
Let the nations commit themselves
          to your Plan!

Psalm 10

Why do You seem so far from me,
        O Silent One?
Where do You hide when fears
        beset me?
I boast and strike out against
        those weaker than myself,
        even knowing I shall be caught in
        a snare of my own making.

When I feel insecure,
        I look for pleasure,
        greed grips my heart and I
        banish You from my life.
In my pride, I seek You not,
I come to believe, "I am the Creator
        of the world."

I even prosper at times:
        your Love seems too great for me,
        out of my reach;
        as for my fears, I pretend they
        do not exist.
I think in my heart, "I do not need
        You;
        adversity will come only to others."

My eyes watch carefully for another's
        weakness,
I wait in secret like a spider
        in its web;
I wait that I might seize those who

are weaker than myself,
draw others into my web,
that I might use them to
feel powerful.

Like me, the fearful are crushed,
we fall by our own doubts.
Then we think in our hearts,
"I do not deserve Love;
my Beloved has forgotten me,
I am alone with my fears forever."

Awaken, O Love! O You who created me,
return to my side;
forget me not in my weakness.
Why do I turn my back to You,
and say in my heart, "You will
not take notice of me?"
You do see me. Yes, you know of
my anguish and fears,
that You may take me once again
unto yourself;
When I commit myself into your hands,
You are ever my strength and comforter.

Break then the webs I have woven,
Seek out all my fears
until You find not one.
You are my Beloved for ever and ever;
all that is broken within me
will be made whole.

O my Beloved, You hear my deepest
desires;

You will strengthen my heart,
       You will answer my prayer;
That I might live with integrity
And become a loving presence in the world!

Psalm 11

In the Beloved do I make my retreat.
       How can you say to me,
       "Flee like a bird to the
                mountains;
       for lo, the unloving bend the bow,
       fitting their arrow to the string;
       they aim to destroy what is good?"
If the foundations of goodness are
                undermined,
       what will remain?

The Beloved dwells in the Holy Temple,
       the sacred place within our hearts;
       loving and testing each one of us.
Divine Love offers both the good
                and the unloving
       opportunities to grow,
                to become whole,
       enduring with Love those who
                choose the way of darkness.

Those who walk without light
       will know fear and doubt;

ignorance will be their guide.
For our Creator is just, gifting us
      with free will;
Those who walk in the Light
      will behold the Beloved's face.

Psalm 12

Come to our aid, O Beloved!
      darkness seems to pervade the earth;
Where is the faith, the integrity
      that once lived in the hearts
         of your people?
Where is the truth, the trust
      that made its home in us?

O Love, cleanse us from our double talk,
Create in us new and single hearts,
Spare us from those who think,
      "Our speeches will win over all.
      Words are our weapons;
      no one can master us!"

"For the hearts of those who call to Me,
For those who cry out for wholeness,
I shall now make Myself known,"
      says the Beloved;

"I shall make Myself known in their
        hearts."

The promises of Love are pure,
        like silver refined in a crucible,
        like gold purified seven times.
Be our safeguard, O Blessed One,
Stay close by throughout these dark days
        where unloving hearts seem to abound.
Come to our aid, O Beloved!

Psalm 13

How long, my Beloved?
        Will you forget me forever?
How long will you hide your
        face from me?
How long must I bear this pain
        in my soul,
        and live with sorrow
        all the day?
How long will fear rule my life?

Notice my heart and answer me,
        O my Beloved;
        enlighten me, lest I walk as
        one dead to life;

Lest my fears say,
"We have won the day;"
Lest they rejoice in their strength.

As I trust in your steadfast
Love;
my heart will rejoice,
for in You is freedom.
I shall sing to the Beloved,
who has answered my prayers
a thousand fold!
Come, O Beloved, make your home
in my heart.

Psalm 14

The hearts of fools say,
"There is no power in Love."
They are ignorant; they torture
themselves and others;
They walk in utter darkness
calling it light.

Love looks into the heart
of every person,
to see if any act with wisdom,
if any seek to walk with Love.

Many there are who have gone
          astray,
     who are ruled by greed and power.
Is there one who is wise and kind?

Have they no knowledge,
          all the ignorant,
     who devour people and nations
          as if they were bread,
     and never call upon Love?
Terror will reign in their hearts;
     for Love's friend is Truth
     and in Truth will those
          who seek Love's way
          be set free.

O that the hearts of Love's
          children
     might wrestle with angels!
O that they might rejoice in life,
     in the abundance of Love's gifts!

Psalm 15

O Beloved, whom will You invite
    into the abode of your Heart?
Who will dwell with You in Love?

One who walks with integrity, who
    is in harmony with your Word,
        and sings the heart's song;
Whose tongue speaks truth
    judging not others and
    seeking only the good;
Whose eyes behold not the outer
        garments of the body,
    but see within the inner robe
    of Love;
Whose own weaknesses are acknowledged
    and brought to light in prayer;
Who is just in all affairs of life
    and takes not advantage of
        another.

One who does all these things,
    will join the Dance of Life!
    will sing the Song of Joy!

Psalm 16

Remain ever before me,
        O Living Presence,
    for in You am I safe.
You are my Beloved; in You
    I can do all things.

I look to those who are at one
        with You and
    learn from them of your ways;
My delight increases each time
    I sense your presence
        within me!
Songs of praise well up from
    my heart!

Love is my chosen food, my cup,
    holding me in its power.
Where I have come from,
Where'er I shall go,
    Love is my birthright,
        my true estate.

I bless the Counselor who guides
    my way;
    in the night also does my heart
    instruct me.
I walk beside the Spirit of Truth;
    I celebrate the Light.

Thus my heart is glad, and my soul
    rejoices;

I shall not be afraid,
    nor fall into the pit of despair;
In Love's presence there is fullness
        of joy.

You are my Beloved; in You
        will I live!

Psalm 17

Listen to my heart, O Love Divine;
        hear the cry within me!
Heed my prayer from lips that
        would utter truth!
For in You do I seek justice!
Be Thou my eyes that I may
        see with clarity.

If You try my heart,
        if You visit me by night,
        if You test me, You will
            discover
        I desire only to draw closer
            to You.
I look at the injustice and the
            oppression
        that dwell in your land;

Be Thou my feet that I may walk
          along your paths;
     that I may be a benevolent
          presence on life's highway.

I call upon You knowing You will
          answer me,
          Heart of my heart;
     incline your ear to me,
          hear my words.
Wondrously show your steadfast love,
O Love Divine, who walks beside me
     giving me strength to meet
     the fears that dwell within.

Keep me the apple of your eye;
     hide me in the shadow of your
          wings,
          from all that would separate me
          from your love.

Open my heart that compassion may
          be my companion;
Where I meet pride, humble me;
Where I meet anger, calm my fears;
Where I meet injustice, cause me
          to act in love's way.
May I be as gentle as the doe,
     as fearless as the lion,
     as faithful as the dog.

Arise, O Divine Love!
     confront all within me
     that is not whole!

Deliver me from deadly fears
        and doubts,
    shine your Light into my darkness.
May my heart receive the bounty of
        your Love,
May my children and their children
    walk with You in gratitude
        and joy.

For I shall behold your face
        in Truth,
    when I am fully awake,
I shall dwell in the house of
    love and peace and joy!

$\mathcal{P}$salm 18

I abandon myself to You, O Living Presence,
        my strength.
You are my rock, my stronghold,
        my freedom,
    Almighty One, the rock and
        foundation of my life,
    Just One, tower of strength,
        the source of truth and light,
I call upon You, Heart of my heart,
        singing praises to your Name,
    and fear no longer holds me.

The demons of darkness assailed me,
the blindness of ignorance led me
astray;
The shadows of fear paralyzed me,
the anguish of loneliness
confronted me.
In my distress I called out to You,
O Gracious One;
to You I cried for help.
You heard my voice, O Loving Presence,
You harkened to my cry.

Then did You, O Divine Presence, show
unto me a vision:
the earth reeled and rocked;
the foundations of the mountains
trembled
and quaked, as if to slough off
the ravages of destruction
perpetrated by greedy hands.
On the wings of the wind, You did come,
with darkness a covering
around You,
a canopy of thick clouds
dark with water.
Out of the brightness before You
there broke through the clouds
hailstones,
coals of fire lept from
the mountaintops.
As your voice uttered in the heavens,
thunder and lightning stormed
the earth;

like arrows from a bow,
      the peoples scattered.

Yet there was no safe haven,
      no hiding place from fear.
Then the channels of the sea were seen,
      and the foundations of the world
         laid bare,
The earth gave a mighty shudder
      then settled down to heal in
         the Silence.

O Compassionate One, You reached
      from on high, You took me,
      You drew me out of many waters.
You delivered me from the fears
      that bound me, and
      from ignorance that blinded me;
      for they threatened to overcome me,
      to separate me from You.
They came upon me when I looked not
      to You;
      yet You, O Merciful One, were
      ever present.
You brought me forth into the Light;
You released my fears, You delighted
      in me.

O Holy One, You see the intentions
      of my heart;
      As I surrender to your love,
      I grow in peace and gratitude.
For to lose my life is to find Life;
      O keep me steadfast in love

for You, Life of my life!
The spirit of your Word is ever
before me,
the Counselor ever present to
guide me.
I pray for a clean heart, O Beloved,
to be free from guilt.
May I walk with You justly, with mercy
and in peace,
a mirror of your love in the world.

Those who love truth will see your Light;
Those who walk in justice, will see
your Mercy;
Those who live with integrity, will see
You in all they meet;
But those whose path is crooked,
who walk on the low road,
will live in the shadows of fear.
The humble are always close to You,
the haughty, too distracted
to see,
will one day fall.

Yes, You are the Light of my life;
You shine through my darkness.
Yes, with You I can do all things;
and my spirit soars like
an eagle.
Your ways lead to wholeness,
O Loving Presence;
Your Word in me is life;
How tenderly You live in my heart!

For who is our Creator, but
            the source of Love!
        And who is Life, except
            the Divine Presence!—
You, who gird me with strength,
        and lead me in the way
            of Truth.
You make my feet like hinds' feet,
        and set me secure on the heights.
You teach me the way of justice,
        that I might speak out against
            oppression.
You give me a hunger for silence,
        that I might know the power
            of prayer,
        and You support me in solitude.
You give me freedom to choose the
            journey road;
        I elect the narrow way.
For I pursued my fears and faced them;
        and did not run back until
            I was free.
I saw each one through, so that they
            were not able to rise;
        they were transformed by love.
For You enabled me with strength
            to look deep within;
        holding me when fears threatened
            to overwhelm me.

You brought forgiveness into the
            darkness,
        and softened my heart to forgive
            my adversaries.

Though my fears rose up, as old friends
              being betrayed,
       Love brought them down.
What had been weakness and weeds,
       now turned to strength and roses;
       yes, my fears were redeemed by Love.
You delivered me from prejudice and
              intolerance;
       You opened my heart to all nations;
       people whom I had not known
              befriended me.
As soon as they beheld the radiance
              of your love,
       they came to my door;
       strangers came desiring to
              hear your Word.
Yes, strangers came—and those who had
       separated themselves from Love,
       they came seeking release from
              their fears.

The Most High lives; blessed be
              my Rock,
       and exalted be the Heart of
              my heart,
The Loving One, who helped me face
              my fears
       and opened my heart to the poor;
Who delivered me out of the darkness
              of ignorance;
       Yes, You did bring victory over
              my fears;
       You led me into harmony and
              wholeness.

For this I will extol You, O my Beloved,
among the nations,
and sing praises to your Name.
Peace, gratitude, love, and assurance are
gifts bestowed by Love.
May all peoples live in your Truth
in the land of peace forever.
Amen.

Psalm 19

The heavens declare the glory
of the Creator;
the firmament proclaims the
handiwork of Love.
Day to day speech pours forth
and night to night knowledge
is revealed.
There is no speech,
nor are there words;
their voice is not heard;
Yet does their music go out
through all the earth,
and their words to the end
of the world.

In them a tent for the sun is set,
        which is like a bride and groom
            on their wedding night
        as they sing love's song and
            celebrate the dance of life.
Its rising is in eternity,
        and its circuit to infinity;
There is nothing hid from the
            sunlight.

The law of Love is perfect,
        reviving the soul;
The testimony of Love is sure,
        making wise the simple;
The precepts of Love are right,
        rejoicing the heart;
The authority of Love is pure,
        enlightening the eyes;
The spirit of Love is wondrous,
        enduring forever;
The rites of Love are true,
        awakening compassion.

More to be desired are they
            than gold,
        even much fine gold;
Sweeter also than honey and
        drippings of the honeycomb.
Moreover by them are the loving
            alerted;
        in keeping them there is
            great reward.

But who can discern their own
weaknesses?
Cleanse me, O Love, from
all my hidden faults.
Keep me from boldly acting in
error;
let my fears not have dominion
over me!
Then shall I become a beneficial
presence,
freely and fully surrendered
to your Love.

Let the words of my mouth
and the meditation of my heart
find favor in your Heart
O my Beloved, my strength and
my joy!

Psalm 20

May the One who created you in
wholeness
meet your needs when you
call!
May the Name of Love be your
protection
and rise up in your heart as a

tower of strength!
May all you have given in gratitude
and with open hands
be returned to you a hundredfold!
May your heart's desires and all
your plans
be fulfilled in due season!
Let us shout for joy as Love
triumphs over fear;
Let our thankful hearts sing
in loud acclamation to the
Beloved,
who answers our heartfelt
prayers!

Now I know that Love comes to all
who open their hearts, and
dwells therein
offering gifts of peace and
harmony.
Some may boast of wealth and
personal power;
they will stumble and fall.
Let us boast of the One who
comes in the Name of Love;
We shall rise up strong and sure.

O Beloved, You who have created us,
hear our call,
make your home in our hearts!

Psalm 21

In your strength I rejoice,
   O my Beloved,
  and in your Presence
   my heart finds rest!
You heed the heart's desire,
  answering the cry of the soul,
  and You bestow blessing upon
   blessing;
Your Love is as a crown of fine
   gold upon my head.
I asked for life; and life
   you did provide,
  eternal life comes through
   your Love.
All glory be yours, O Loving Presence,
  splendor and majesty are
   your raiment.
Yes, your blessings are forever;
  You delight me with the joy
   of your Presence.
Forever I will put my trust in You;
  and as I abandon myself to You
   in love,
  I am assured of peace.

You root out my fears; standing
  firm beside me as I face
   the shadows within.
Like a blazing sun your light shines.
My fears flee from your sight;
  your fire consumes them.

Generations to come will sing to
      your glory
In gratitude and joy for your
      saving power.
For You put fears to flight, that
      love and justice might reign.

All praise be yours, O Wondrous One!
      forever will I sing and honor
      your saving grace.

Psalm 22

O my Beloved, why have You
      forsaken me?
Why are You so far, abandoning me
      as I groan in misery?
O my Beloved, I cry by day, but
      You do not answer;
      and by night, but find no rest.

Yet You are holy, praised
      through all generations.
In You our parents trusted;
      they trusted, and You did come
      to their aid.
To You they cried, and were heard;

in You they trusted, and
were not disappointed.

But I seem as nothing, hardly alive;
scorned and despised by many.
Those who see me make fun
at my expense,
they ridicule and gossip
among themselves;
"Commit yourself to the Most High;
let Love deliver you,
you who delight in the Most High!"

Yet, You are the One who took me
from the womb;
You kept me safe upon my
mother's breasts.
Upon You I was cast from my birth,
and ever since my mother bore me,
You have been my strength.
Come close to me, for trouble is near
and there is none to help.

Many, like bulls, surround me,
they come at me with great force.
With fire in their eyes
and bellowing roars,
they charge at me.

I am poured out like water,
and all my bones are weak;
my heart is like wax,
melting within my breast;

My strength is broken as a
          shard of pottery,
        and my mouth is dry;
        You have laid me in the dust
          of death.

Yes, boars are round about me;
        a company of evildoers encircle me;
        they have pierced my hands and feet—
I can count all my bones—
        they stare and gloat over me
          awaiting my demise;
They divide my belongings among
          them,
        avariciously casting lots.

But You, O Beloved, be not far off!
        You, who are my help, hasten to
          my aid!
Free my soul from this agony,
        my life from the power of
          the boar!
Save me from the mouth of
          the lion,
        my afflicted soul from the
          horns of the bull!

I will tell of your Name to
          all I meet,
        in the midst of assemblies
          I will praise You;
You, who are in wonder of the Mystery,
          give praise!
For our loving Creator does not turn
        away from the afflicted,
And does not hide from them;

But their cries are heard,
        their prayers rise up to heaven.

To You, O Beloved, I lift up my voice
            in the great congregation;
        for You promise to remain with
            those whose love is steadfast.
The hungry shall eat and be
            satisfied;
Those who seek You shall sing praises!
Your Heart our dwelling place forever!

All the ends of the earth shall
            remember
        and turn to Love's way;
And all the families of the nations
        shall bow down with grateful
            hearts.
For power and authority belong to
        the Most High,
    who rules over the nations.

Yes, to the Most High shall all the
            proud of the earth be humbled;
        before the Creator shall all bow
            who go down to the dust,
        and who cannot sustain their lives.
Posterity shall know and serve Love,
        telling of the One who abides in all
            to the coming generations,
And proclaiming deliverance to a
            people yet unborn
        that the Most High dwells among us.

Psalm 23

O my Beloved, you are my shepherd,
      I shall not want;
You bring me to green pastures
            for rest
            and lead me beside still waters
                  renewing my spirit,
            You restore my soul.
You lead me in the path of
            goodness
            to follow Love's way.

Even though I walk through the
            valley of the shadow and
                  of death,
      I am not afraid;
For You are ever with me;
            your rod and your staff
                  they guide me,
            they give me strength
                  and comfort.

You prepare a table before me
            in the presence of all my fears;
                  you bless me with oil,
                  my cup overflows.
Surely goodness and mercy will
                  follow me
            all the days of my life;
and I shall dwell in the heart
            of the Beloved
                  forever.

Psalm 24

The earth is yours, O Giver of Life,
      in all its fulness and glory,
      the world and all those who
         dwell therein;
For You have founded it upon
        the seas,
      and established it upon
        the rivers.

Who shall ascend your hill,
        O Gracious One?
      and who shall stand in your
        holy place?
All who have clean hands and
        pure hearts,
      who do not lift up their souls
        to what is false,
      nor make vows deceitfully.
All these will be blessed by the
        Heart of Love,
      and renewed through forgiveness.
Such is the promise to those
      who seek Love's face.

Lift up your heads, O gates!
      and be lifted up,
        O ancient doors!
      that the Compassionate One
        may come in.
Who is the Compassionate One?
      the Beloved, strong and steadfast,

the Beloved, firm and sure!
Lift up your heads, O gates!
     and be lifted up,
          O ancient doors!
     that the Compassionate One
          may come in!
Who is this Compassionate One?
     the Beloved, Heart of your heart,
          Life of your life,
     this is the Compassionate One!

Psalm 25

To You, O Love, I lift up my soul;
O Heart within my heart,
     in You I place my trust.
     Let me not feel unworthy;
     let not fear rule over me.
Yes! let all who open their hearts
     savor You and bless the earth!

Compel me to know your ways, O Love;
     instruct me upon your paths.
Lead me in your truth,
          and teach me,
     for through You will I know
          wholeness;

I shall reflect your light
        both day and night.

I know of your mercy, Compassionate One,
        and of your steadfast love.
    You have been with me
        from the beginning.
Forgive the many times I have
    walked away from You
    choosing to walk alone.
With your steadfast love,
        once again,
Companion me along your way.

You are gracious and just,
        O Spirit of Truth,
    happy to guide those who
        miss their way;
You enjoy teaching all who are open,
    all who choose to live in truth.
Your paths are loving and sure,
        O Holy One,
    for those who give witness to You
        through their lives.

For the honor of your Name,
        O Beloved,
    forgive my separation from You.
I bow down before You;
        instruct me, that I might choose
            the way of love and truth.
I would live in your abundance,
    and my children as well.
Your friendship is offered to all

whose hearts are open;
    You will make known your promises
        to them.
My eyes are ever on You, Beloved,
    keep my feet from stumbling
        along the way.

Turn to me, O Holy One, and envelop me
        with your love, for
    I am lonely and oppressed.
Relieve the blocks in my heart
    that keep me separated from You;
See all the darkness within me;
    fill it with your healing light.
Look at my pain and all my fears;
    they shut out love and life.

Protect me and free me;
    let me not live as unworthy,
    for I would make my home in You.
May integrity and wholeness fill me
    as I dwell with You,
        O Loving Presence.

O Beloved, as you renew me,
    redeem the nations,
That we on earth may unfold
        your Plan.

Psalm 26

Speak on my behalf, O Beloved,
    for I would choose the path
        of wholeness,
    trusting in your love
        without reserve.
    May my heart be as your Heart;
    May my mind be as your Mind—
As your steadfast love guides me,
As I live in faithfulness to You.

I walk with friends of integrity,
    and associate with those
        who live in truth;
I love the company of faith-filled
        people,
    And count myself among those
        who make your Word their own.

Cleanse my heart in innocence
    that I might childlike be,
Singing songs of thanksgiving
    and proclaiming the
        Beloved's way.

O Loving Presence, I cherish your
        dwelling place, my heart;
    O, that I might radiate Love Divine;
Keep me always in your presence,
Ever-ready to praise your Name.
Make me holy, complete in You,
Write my name among the saints.

For I would choose the path
        of wholeness;
Fulfill your promise and be gracious
        to me.
Then, standing with equanimity in
        heaven's company,
I shall ever bless You,
        O Beloved of my heart.

Psalm 27

Love is my light and
        my salvation,
        whom shall I fear?
Love is the strength of
        my life,
Of whom shall I be afraid?

When fears assail me,
        rising up to accuse me,
Each one in turn shall be seen
        in Love's light.
Though a multitude of demons
        rise up within me,
        my heart shall not fear.
Though doubts and guilt do battle,
        yet shall I remain confident.

One thing have I asked of Love,
    that I shall ever seek:
That I might dwell in the
        Heart of Love
    all the days of my life,
To behold the Beauty of my Beloved,
    and to know Love's Plan.

For I shall hide in Love's heart
    in the day of trouble,
As in a tent in the desert,
Away from the noise of my fears.
And I shall rise above
    my struggles, my pain,
Shouting blessings of gratitude
    in Love's Heart
And singing melodies of praise
    to my Beloved.

Hear, O my Beloved,
    when I cry aloud,
    be gracious and answer me!
You have said, "Seek my face."
    My heart responds,
"Your face, my Beloved, do I seek;
    hide not your face from me."

Do not turn from me,
    You who have been my refuge.
Enfold me in your strong arms,
    O Blessed One.
Though my father and mother
    may not understand me,
You, my Beloved, know me and love me.

Teach me to be love,
            as You are Love;
Lead me through each fear;
Hold my hand as I walk through
            valleys of doubt each day,
That I may know your peace.

I believe that I shall know the
            Realm of Heaven,
        of Love, here on Earth!
Wait for the Beloved,
        be strong with courage
            of the heart;
Yes! Wait for the Beloved of
            your heart!

Psalm 28

Heart of my heart, I call to You;
You hear my cry and support me.
Should You remain silent in me,
I walk as in a desert waste.
You heed the voice of my humble request
        when I call your holy Name,
        when I lift my hands,
            O Holy One,
        to acknowledge your power and glory.

Protect me from those who love
           You not,
     those who delight in their own law,
Whose words become meaningless
           by the deeds of their hearts.
In your justice, they will reap
           the harvest of iniquity;
In your mercy, they will receive
           a reward worthy of their acts.
For they, who remain separated
           from your love, O Beloved,
Will miss the joy of your
                     saving grace,
           the peace of your companioning
                     Presence.

Blessed are You, Heart of my heart!
           for You heed the cry of my spirit.
You are my strength and my protection;
           into your hands I commend my soul.
My heart leaps as You come to my aid,
                     and my lament becomes
           a song of exultation,
           a shout of praise to You,
                     O my Comforter!

Remember well, O my friends,
The Spirit of Truth becomes known
           to all who are receptive to Love,
                     giving strength and shelter.
Mercy and justice are our birthright—
Let us call on the Giver of Life
           to guide our feet into the
                     way of peace,

to live in our hearts forever.
Blessed be the Name of the Most High!

Psalm 29

Give praise to the Beloved,
    O heavenly hosts,
Sing of Love's glory and strength.
Exalt the glory of Love's Name;
Adore the Beloved in holy splendor.

The voice of the Beloved is upon
            the waters;
Love's voice echoes over the oceans
            and seas.
The voice of Love is powerful,
    majestic is the voice of Love.

The voice of the Beloved breaks the
            bonds of oppression,
    shatters the chains of injustice.
Love invites all to the dance of freedom,
    to sing the Beloved's song of truth.

The voice of Love strikes with fire
            upon hearts of stone.
The voice of Love uproots the thorns

of fear,
Love uproots fear in every open
    heart.

The voice of Love is heard in every storm,
    and strips the ego bare;
And in their hearts all cry,
    "Glory!"

The Beloved lives in our hearts;
    Love dwells with us forever.
May Love give strength to all people!
May Love bless all nations with peace!

Psalm 30

I will praise You, O my Beloved,
    for You have raised me up,
    and have not let my fears
        overwhelm me.
O Compassionate One, I cried
        for help, and You
        comforted me.
You, Love, released my soul
        from despair,
    restored me to life from among
        those who live in fear.

Sing praises to the Beloved,
> O you saints,
>> and give thanks to Love's holy Name.
Love withdraws when we close our hearts,
> yet ever awaits an open door.
In the evening we may weep,
> yet joy comes with the morning.

In my prosperity, I had lost sight
> of Love,
>> I found power in my wealth.
In your mercy, O Beloved, my foundations
> You shook,
>> And, in recognizing my separation
>> from You,
>> I was dismayed.

I cried to You for help; to You,
> I pleaded for forgiveness:
>> "What profit in my riches if
>> I am separated from Love?
>> Will emptiness praise You?
Will it tell of your faithfulness?
Hear, O my Beloved, and be gracious to me!
> O Love, come to my assistance!"

And You turned my mourning into dancing;
> You set me free and
>> clothed me with gladness.
Now my soul may praise You and not be silent.
O my Beloved, I will be grateful to You
> forever and ever.
>> Amen.

Psalm 31

In You, Beloved, I would make my home;
Though I be humiliated with guilt,
      Your mercy and forgiveness will
         deliver me!
Hear me and hasten to my assistance!
For You are my strength and have the power
         to raise me up!

Yes, You are strength and truth to me;
      lead me and guide me
         that I may grow;
Loosen me from the net which entangles
      me,
      for your Heart is my home.
Into your hands I commend my soul;
      You have redeemed me, O Love,
         Faithful One.

You turn from those who trust
         in false idols;
      I put my trust in You, O Beloved.
I rejoice and am glad for your
         steadfast Love,
      for You have seen my guilt,
      You have noted my wrongdoings,
And have not left me alone with my fears;
      Rather, You have set my feet on
         the path of love.

Be gracious to me, Beloved, for I am
         in distress;

my eyes are dim from weeping,
    my soul is deep with grief.
For my life is worn away with sorrow,
    and my years with sighing;
My body has weakened and my bones
        waste away with misery.

All my fears rise up to mock me,
    my neighbors turn away,
My friends dread to see me and
    flee from my sickness of soul.
My mind, too, has left me
        like one who is dead;
I have become like a broken vessel.
Yes, I hear the voices around me
    whispering of my plight—
    fears rise up on every side!
Isolation, rejection, fear surround me
    and conspire to overwhelm me.

Still, I trust in You, O Love,
    I repeat, "You are my Life."
My life is in your hands;
    deliver me from the fears which
        separate me!
Let your face shine on me;
    save me in your steadfast love!
Let me know your forgiveness,
        O Love,
    for I call upon You;
    let my fears be cast out,
        let them be transformed.
Let me speak only truth, Beloved,
    that I might live with integrity,
        offering songs of praise to You.

O how abundant is your goodness,
which is ever-present to those
who reverence You,
and available to all who make
your Heart their home,
openly for all to see!
Like a mother hen, You shelter them
from temptations of the world;
You hold them safe under your wings
from the enemy ... fear.

Blessed be the Beloved,
Who has wondrously shown
steadfast love to me
when I was beset by an army of fear.
I had said in my fright,
"I am separated from your love."
And you heard my pleas
when I cried to You for help.

Listen in the Silence, all you saints!
The Beloved upholds the faith-filled,
but those who separate themselves from
truth and goodness,
know not Love.
So, be strong, and let your heart take
courage,
all you, who would know Love!

Psalm 32

Blessed is each one whose wrongdoings
                have been forgiven,
        whose shame has been forgotten.
Blessed is each one in whom Love Divine
                finds a home,
        and whose spirit radiates truth.

When I acknowledged not my shortcomings,
        I became ill through all my defenses.
And day and night, guilt weighed heavy
                in my heart;
My spirit became dry as desert bones.

I admitted my faults to the Most High,
        and I made known my regret;
I cried out, "Forgive me, O Comforter,
        for those times I have sinned in
                my thoughts, my words,
                and my deeds;"
And the Beloved created a clean heart
        within me.

Therefore, let everyone who is sincere
        give thanks to the Beloved;
For whenever we feel overwhelmed
                by fear,
        we shall be embraced by Love.
Dwelling in the heart of the Beloved,
        we are free from distress,
                free to live creatively.

O my Beloved, you are my guide and
          my teacher;
Be watchful of me, give me your
          counsel.
I pray for the gifts of inner peace
          and wisdom,
For the gift of reverence for life.

Many are the heartaches of those
          separated from Love;
Steadfast love abides with those
       who surrender their lives into
          the hands of the Beloved.
Be glad and rejoice, all you
       who walk along the path of truth!
And shout for joy, all you upright
          of heart!

Psalm 33

Rejoice in the Beloved, O you holy ones!
       Praise is a grace of the loving.
Praise the Beloved with strings and reeds,
Give praise with dance and leaps;
          sing a new song, and
          shout with joyful heart!

For the word of the Creator is truth,
　　and all creation reflects the
　　　　faithfulness of the Beloved.
Justice and mercy we render to the Holy One,
To the universe filled with Love Divine.

By the Word of the Beloved,
　　the heavens were made,
And all who dwell on earth
　　　　by the Creator's breath.
All creation, from the distant stars
　　to the depth of the seas,
Is held together by Love.

May all the earth reverence the Beloved,
　　may everyone stand in awe of
　　　　Love!
For when the Beloved speaks,
　　it comes to pass;
As Love's way guides and directs,
　　thus, it stands.

Without Love, the nations' counsel
　　　　comes to nothing,
　　the plans of the people are futile.
The counsel of the Creator is eternal
　　available to every generation.
Blessed are the nations who hear
　　the Word and abide in it;
All people who respond to the Beloved!

For, the Beloved dwells in every heart
　　that is open and free;
Into our hands, into our hearts,
　　does the Beloved surrender,
　　　　that we might do with Love

what we will.
Do we not know, that the nations
        are not saved by military might,
        just as generals are not
                saved by their own strength?
All such arms are the outward expression
                of greed in fearful hearts;
They will reap only despair and
        destruction.

Behold, the love of the Beloved is stronger
        then ten thousand bombs,
        more to be desired than the wealth
        of all nations.
Do we not know that to dwell in the
        heart of the Beloved
Is the promise to every nation,
        the birthright of all people,
        the journey to life eternal?

Our soul yearns for the Beloved,
        for peace, joy, and assurance.
Yes, our hearts are glad and sing
        songs of gratitude,
Praising the name of the Holy One!
May every nation come to live in
        the steadfast love of
                the Spirit of Truth!
May every people hope in Love Divine!

Psalm 34

I will bless the Beloved at all times;
     a song of praise will I sing.
My soul speaks to the Beloved continually;
     let all who suffer hear and be glad.
O, open your hearts, friends,
       that your pain and loneliness
         be turned to Love;
And then, we shall rejoice in the Beloved
       together!

When I searched for Love, the Beloved
       answered within my heart,
       and all my fears flew away.
Look to the Beloved, and your
         emptiness will be filled,
       your face will radiate Love.
For when you cry, the Beloved hears
         and comes to you,
       your troubles disappear.
The Beloved sends angels to those
         who call on Love
       to awaken them from their fears.
         O taste and see!
The Beloved is within you!

Happy are all who dwell in the
         Beloved's heart!
Abandon yourself into Love's hands,
       O you holy ones,
For those who give themselves to
       the Beloved,

lack no good thing.
Everyone separated from Love is empty
         and hungry within;
But those who open their hearts to
         the Beloved,
         are filled to overflowing!

O come and see, come and hear,
         how we honor the Beloved.
Many there are who desire Life,
         who yearn for fulfillment,
         who covet the wisdom of Truth.
Keep your heart open and free,
         make time to dwell in Silence,
Become a peaceful presence in the world.
For the Beloved sees the deeds
                  of our hearts, and
         hears our inmost thoughts.
The face of the Beloved turns from
         the evil ways of men and women;
For Love is kind and merciful and
                  remembers not our sins.
Rather, the Beloved is patient,
         ever-waiting for us to cry out
                  for forgiveness,
         to embrace Love's way.
How often the Beloved weeps with
                  compassion
         over those who are crushed in spirit.

Though we are beset with many fears
         that cause illness and troubles,
The Beloved is ever ready
         to lighten our heavy hearts,

to ease our burdens,
to comfort us in our sorrows.
The Beloved renews the life of all
who surrender to Love.

Psalm 35

Pray on my behalf, O Beloved, for those
who fight against me;
Forgive on my behalf those who abuse me!
Pour forth your strength into my heart
that I might stand strong!
Encircle with healing love those
who persecute me through fear!
And say to my soul,
"I am with you always!"

Melt the hearts of stone in those
Who seek to kill my body, my spirit.
Turn them around and let them delight
in your way.
Let their ignorance become as chaff
before the wind,
send angels to lead them home to You.
Let their path become filled with light
that they may see the way of truth!

For without cause they have tried to
                ensnare me;
        without cause they threaten my life.
Surprise them, O Love, with joy!
For ignorance cannot live where your
                love abides;
Let them rise up with a new conscience
        and regret their past acts
                against others.

Then, O Love, my soul shall rejoice,
        exulting in your goodness.
My whole being shall say,
        "O Beloved, who is like You,
You who give strength to the weak,
                praying on their behalf,
        when fear threatens to overwhelm them,
        holding them back from retaliation
                through your saving love?"

False witnesses rise up, asking me
        questions I cannot answer.
They return my kindness with cruelty;
                my soul weeps.
Yet I, when they were afflicted—
        I lit prayer candles,
        I fasted and sent them help.
I prayed in my simple way as though
        grieving for my family or
                a friend;
I acted as one who grieves a dying mother,
        bowed down and in mourning.

Yet when I stumbled and needed assistance,
        they gathered about me with glee,

they turned against me;
Even strangers whom I did not know,
        mocked me day and night;
They seemed to gather strength in
                denouncing me,
        and became all the more violent.

How long, O Beloved, must I endure this?
        Rescue me from the oppressors,
        my life from the lions!
I long to give thanks in the great assembly,
        to praise You wherever people gather.

Fill those who rejoice over my plight
                with compassion,
Let peace come to those who hate me
                without cause.
For many desire conflict and war,
        and turn against those who are quiet
                in the land,
        they are driven by greed.
By speaking against me saying, "Aha,
                you are to blame."
        they think to hide their own deceit.

You have seen it all, O Love;
                be silent no longer!
Beloved, stay close beside me!
Hear me, and rise up on my behalf,
        let justice and peace reign!
Yes, O Compassionate One, let truth
                and love overcome ignorance,
                according to your goodness;
        that all might rejoice and give thanks!

Foolish are they to think that persecution
       will bring them joy;
Nor will destruction bring them peace.

Let those who rejoice in another's misfortune,
       in their shame become contrite;
Let them be humbled and turn their hearts
              to You, O Beloved,
       all those who know not Love!
May all who offer their lives to peace
       shout for joy and be glad,
              and always pray,
       "Great are You, O Love,
       Who dwell in all open hearts!"
Then shall I sing of your saving justice
       and praise You all day long!

Psalm 36

Ignorance lives deep in the hearts
       of those who know not Love;
There is no reverence for Truth
              before their eyes.
For they see themselves as powerful
       and are too proud to see how
              they deceive themselves and others.
They speak not with integrity and

act not with wisdom and love.
At night their thoughts turn to
                    plotting,
          driving them to seek more power;
          fear becomes their constant companion.

Would that they knew that your steadfast
                    love, O Holy One,
                    extends to the heavens,
          your faithfulness to all the world.
Your saving justice is like the mountains,
                    firm and sure,
                    your judgments are like the
                    mighty deep;
Your love supports all of creation;
                    Your love is everlasting.

How precious is your steadfast love,
                    O Companioning Presence.
We, your children, take refuge in
                    the shadow of your wings.
We feast on the abundance of Gaia,
                    the Earth;
                    You invite us to drink from living
                    streams.
For in You is the very source of life;
          and in your Light do we see light.

May your steadfast love endure to those
                    who know You,
          your saving grace to those
                    who love truth and justice!
Protect us from the seeds of arrogance;
          the weeds of greed drive away.

Open the hearts of those who live in
      darkness, O Beloved,
    that they might rise up and live
      in your Light.

Psalm 37

Give no heed to those who are greedy,
    attend not to those who do wrong.
For, like the green grass of spring,
    they soon fade and wither away.

Trust in the Most High, and seek goodness;
    live harmoniously upon the earth
      in peace and with assurance.
Take delight in the Beloved,
    enjoy the bountiful gifts of Love.

Commit your life to the Beloved,
    confident that Love will act
      on your behalf,
Making clear your pathway,
    bright as the sun at midday.

Be still before the Beloved, and wait
    patiently in the silence;
    pray for those who prosper by

deceitful means,
and for those who live by
their own devises.

Recognize your own anger as unfulfilled
desire, and
lift your thoughts to higher planes;
For those who act out of anger,
separate themselves from Love;
And those who live in harmony,
shall know peace, assurance, gratitude,
and love.

In a little while, those who live with greed,
will prosper no more;
the darkness of ignorance will pass,
as a new dawn enlightens the world.
The lovers of darkness shall perish,
while the humble shall inherit
the earth, and
delight themselves in sharing its
abundance with all.

Those who are greedy plot against the
upright
and rationalize their selfish desires;
Yet, the Beloved watches patiently,
knowing that soon they will stumble
and fall.

The greedy call forth guns and
ammunition,
to bring down the poor and needy,
to murder those who walk in peace.

O, if they only knew that their greed
        will kill their own spirit;
    their hearts will be broken.

How much better is the little of
        those who know Love, than
    the abundance of the greedy ones.
For the spirit of the selfish will
        be broken;
    while those who live in love,
        shall dwell with Love.

Love walks with the upright,
    and their heritage is forever;
In difficult times, they will be assured,
    even in times of famine,
        their spirits will be filled.
But those who live by greed
        will perish;
    Like a refining fire, their deeds
    will burn and vanish away
        in smoke.

Those who are greedy borrow, using
        the assets of others,
    money they cannot pay back;
The upright are generous and give.
Blessed by Love, they know inner peace,
        but the selfish cut themselves
        off from Love.

Our lives come from the Most High
        and Love walks beside those with
        open hearts;

Those who know Love are blessed and
shall be filled with the Spirit;
though their lives may seem difficult,
Love raises them up.

From my birth to my elder years,
I have watched the upright blessed
with inner strength and faith.
Living as beneficial presences in the world,
their children come to know Love.

Turn from ignorance, and become all that
you were born to be;
thus will you fulfill your birthright.
The Beloved loves justice and will enable
all who call upon Love to grow
in love.
The upright of heart will know the
fulness of life,
their children will be blessed.
Those who give greed a home, set
their children on the path that
leads to darkness.

The upright of heart know Silence;
when they speak, it is with
wisdom and justice.
For Love abides in their hearts;
their way is sure.

Those who do wrong look to justify
themselves,
they seek to subdue the upright.

Their greed begets fear and guilt;
    they condemn themselves.
Closing their hearts to Love,
    they live unaware of their own
        deep poverty of heart.

Desire only Love and walk your days
    with the Beloved;
        you will radiate with joy, blessing
        others with Love's presence;
        you will know not loneliness with
        Love's Companioning Presence.

I have seen the greedy ones, their
    ways are overbearing,
    they puff themselves up with pride.
I passed by seeing only an inflated
    balloon,
    a passing fancy soon to be
    brought down.

Look at the innocent, consider those
    honest of heart;
    they leave a rich inheritance
    to their children.
But those who live with greed, end
    their days empty,
    they leave a legacy of hollow vanity
    to their children.

The saving grace of the upright comes
    from the Beloved;

Love is their refuge in times of
trouble.
Love leads the way and they arrive
home safely,
delivered from those who tempt them
with power.
Love invites all to open their hearts.

Psalm 38

O Beloved, in your mercy, forgive me,
raise me up in your compassion!
For arrows of fear pierce my heart,
and guilt weighs heavy upon me.

I live in confusion and despair
because of my anguish;
My body responds with illness
because of my stubbornness.
Ignorance casts me into darkness; and
I grope in every direction,
searching in vain.

Because of foolishness, my heart has
turned to stone,
I am utterly bowed down, overcome
with remorse;
I spend my days in mourning,

and pray for mercy throughout
    the night.
I acknowledge my weakness,
    O Loving Presence,
  illness has overtaken me.
My energy is depleted, my spirit
    crushed;
    I groan under the tumult of
    my heart.

Beloved, all my longing is known to You,
    my sighing is not hidden
    from You.
My heart throbs endlessly, my
    strength fails me;
    even the light of my eyes—
    it also has disappeared.
My friends and companions have
    no time for me,
  my family stays at a distance.

The tempter knows well my weakness
    and lays a snare in my path,
Those who choose the darkness are
    ever at my door,
  seeking my company.

Like someone who is deaf,
    I do not hear,
  like one who is dumb,
    I do not speak.
Yes, I pretend not to hear, because
  I am afraid to rebuke those
    who lead me astray.

For You alone, Beloved, do I wait;
        You alone, O Gracious One, who
            will answer my cry.
And I pray, "Be my strength and
            uphold me,
        when I am weak and about
            to fall!"

For I seem ready to fall,
        my pain is always with me.
I confess my shortcomings,
        I am sorry for my transgression.
With mercy, You shed light
            into my darkness,
I can hide no longer behind the
            shield of ignorance.
Those who choose to live in darkness
        are my adversaries, because
        I choose now to walk in
            the light.

Let me not separate myself from You,
        O Beloved!
    Make your home in my heart!
Roll away the stone from my heart,
        O Love, my Beloved!

Psalm 39

I said, "Be Thou my voice,
    that I may not err with
        my tongue;
I will remain mute, so long
    as my fears assail me."
I was silent in my ignorance,
    I held my peace to no avail;
My distress grew worse,
    my heart burned within me.
As I mused, the fire burned;
    finally, I spoke with my tongue.

"O Loving Presence, be with us
        to the end,
        whatever the measure of our days;
        our life passes as the
            blinking of an eye!
For the gift of life fades too
        soon away,
        yet how precious are we
        in your sight!
Surely your Plan for us is
    written on our hearts!
Surely your angels stand ready
    to guide us on our way!
Surely there is nothing to fear, for
        you abide within us;
        awaiting our awakening to
            your love.

And now, O Loving Presence, for what
do I wait?
My hope is in You.
Forgive me for all my mistakes;
let me not walk in ignorance!
I stand silent before You, I hold
my tongue;
to You I turn in repentance.
Remove the blemishes from my heart;
for I am weary of guilt.
When you blot out the darkness
of sin,
burning it with refining fire,
Surely, I am made new, redeemed by
your love!

Hear my prayer, O Gracious Presence,
and give ear to my cry;
wash away my tears
with your peace!
For I am your passing guest,
a sojourner, as in all
generations.
Look upon me with mercy, that I
may know joy
and live in the realm of Love,
now and in the life to come!"
Amen.

Psalm 40

I waited patiently for the Beloved,
      who came to me and heard
          my cry.
Love raised me from the pits of
         despair,
      out of confusion and fear,
      and set my feet upon a rock,
         making my steps secure.
There is a new song in my mouth,
      a song of praise to the Beloved.
Many will see and rejoice,
      and put their trust in Love.

Blessed are those who make Love
         their home,
      who do not turn to the proud,
      to those who follow false idols!
You have increased, O Beloved,
      your wondrous deeds and your
         thoughts toward us;
      none can compare with You!
Were we to proclaim and tell of your
         saving grace,
      it could not be measured.

Sacrifice and offering are not
         your desire for us;
      for, you have opened our
         heart's ear.
Burnt offerings are not required.
Let us cry out: "Yes, I come;

in the book it is written
of me;
I delight to abandon myself into
your hands,
O my Beloved;
For you are the Heart of my heart."

I tell the glad news of
Love's way
to all who will listen.
Yes, I raise my voice,
with praise and acclamation.
I tell of Love's saving grace
within my heart,
I speak of Love's faithfulness
and healing power.
I do not conceal your steadfast love
and truth
from all whom I meet.
Do not, O Beloved, withhold
your mercy from me,
Let your steadfast love and
faithfulness
ever preserve me!
For fears so often overwhelm me;
My desires and anger cause me
to be blind;
I look away when I see injustice,
my heart becomes cold.

In your mercy, O Beloved, deliver me!
O Love, make haste to help me!
Let my fears be put to rest,
fears that separate me from You;

Let all that keeps me from love,
        from peace and gratitude,
    be transformed within me.

And may all who seek Love
        rejoice and be glad;
May all who would live truth
        and justice,
    continually call upon Love!
As for me, though often broken
        and weak,
    I know that Love dwells within.
As Loving Companion Presence,
        O Beloved,
    You are my hope and my joy!

Psalm 41

Blessed are you who consider the poor!
For you are delivered in the
        day of trouble;
The One who knows all hearts
    protects you and renews
        your life;
    you are called blessed
        in the land;
    you are not beset by fear.

For the Heart of your heart will
              sustain you;
      in illness you will find
          comfort and healing.

As for me, I said, "O Love,
              be gracious to me;
      forgive me, for I have been
          deaf to the cry of the poor."
The fears within me, my enemies,
      hold me prisoner in my
         own house.
When I push them down, deny them,
      they rise up with power;
      I feel so insecure, my
         tongue pours forth lies.
I hear others whisper together
      about me;
      they imagine the worst for me.

They see that fear threatens to
           overwhelm me;
      and will bring about the very
         thing that I fear.
Even my bosom friend in whom
         I trusted,
      who ate of my bread, has
         abandoned me.
Yet will I trust in You, O Love;
           be gracious to me,
      and raise me up, that I may
         conquer my fears!

By this I know that You have
          forgiven me,
     in that my fears have not
          triumphed over me.
For You have upheld me, filled
          me with integrity,
     and opened my heart to the poor.

Blessed be the Beloved, Loving
          Companion Presence,
     from everlasting to everlasting!
          Amen and Amen.

Psalm 42

As a hart longs for flowing streams,
          so longs my soul for You,
               O Beloved.
My soul thirsts for the Beloved,
          for the Living Water.
When may I come and behold
          your face?
Tears have been my only nourishment
          day and night,
While friends ask continually,
          "Where is the Beloved of your
               heart?"

All this I remember,
     as I pour out my soul:
How I knew your Presence within me
     as I went out among the throng,
     proceeding to the House of Prayer;
With loud voice we gave You praise
        and acclamation,
     a multitude proclaiming gratitude
     and joy.
Why are you cast down, O my soul,
     and why are you disquieted
       within me?
My hope is in the Beloved, my
       strength and my joy,
     O my soul, open the door to Love!

My soul is cast down within me,
     therefore I remember You
From my mother's womb to maturity,
     through all the days of my life.
Deep calls to deep
     at the thunder of your waterfalls;
All your waves and your billows
     have washed over me.
By day You lead me in steadfast
       love;
     at night your song is with me,
     prayer from the Heart of my heart.

I say to the Beloved, the Blessed One,
     "Why have You forgotten me?
Why go I mourning because of
       the oppression of fear?"
As with a deadly wound in
       my body,

my fears rise up to taunt me,
saying over and over,
"Where is the Beloved?"

Why are you cast down, O my soul,
and why are you disquieted
within me?
My hope is in the Beloved, my strength
and my joy,
O my soul, open the door to Love!

Psalm 43

Bring justice to the people,
O Beloved,
and strength on my behalf
to stand firm against oppression;
From all that is greedy and unjust
deliver me!
For You are the One in whom I
take refuge;
why have You abandoned me?
Why go I mourning because of the
oppression of ignorance?

O, send out your light and your truth;
let them guide me,

Let them lead me to your holy hill,
  to the home of integrity!
Then will I come to you, Heart of my heart,
  to the Beloved, my exceeding joy;
And I will praise You with song,
  O my Beloved, my Comforter.

Why are you cast down, O my soul,
  and why are you disquieted within me?
My hope is in the Beloved, my strength
   and my joy,
  O my soul, open the door to Love!

Psalm 44

We have heard with our ears,
   O Rock of the ages,
  all generations have proclaimed
The mighty deeds You wrought
   in their days,
  in the days of old;
Of how You with your own hand
   drove out the nations,
  sowing seeds for new life;
Of how You led the peoples
   into bondage,
  and then You set them free;

For not by their own might did
          they win the land,
        nor did their own strength give
          them victory,
But by your power and your might,
        and the light of your countenance;
        for You sought to awaken them!

O, You who know all hearts,
        who are ever-present to your people,
Through You we face our enemies;
        through your Name we call forth
          our fears.
For not in military powers do we trust,
        nor can arms save us.
For You alone can put our fears
          to rest,
        and transform them into peace.
In You, O Gracious One, do we give thanks,
        and forever will we offer You
          our songs of praise.

Yet at times You seem to abandon us,
        leaving us alone with our fears.
You have given us the freedom
          to turn from You;
        and our fears have overwhelmed us.
We become as sheep for slaughter,
        straying far from the fold.
You seem to require too little of us,
        remaining mute as we wander
          on worldly highways.

Without your saving grace, we come in
        conflict with our neighbors,
    we fear all who seem different
        from us.
We seek to better ourselves at the expense
        of other nations,
    we become arrogant and greedy.
All day long we run from our disgrace,
    yet our shame is ever before us,
At the cries of injustice and oppression,
    at the sight of the poor and needy.

As all this comes upon us,
        we remember You, O Infinite Love,
    we pray for your support in
        our conflicts.
Our hearts recall your Word,
    your promises of old,
Yet does deep darkness overshadow us.

Until crises come, we forget the Name
        of the Creator;
    we spread forth our hands to
        a worldly god.
Does not the Most High discover this?
    For the Beloved knows the secrets
        of the heart.
No, Love does not abandon us;
    we ourselves turn our faces
        from the Light.

Rouse yourself! Why do you sleep,
        O foolish peoples?
    Awaken! Do not stray in the darkness
        forever!

Why do you hide your faces?
Why are you ashamed and cast down?
With your souls bowed down to the
dust,
call out to the Beloved for forgiveness.
Rise up, pray for a change of heart!
Then will the Indwelling Companion
Presence
deliver you with steadfast love!

Psalm 45

My heart overflows with gratitude
and peace;
I address my verses to the
Heart of all hearts;
My tongue is like the pen
of a ready scribe.

You are the fairest of all
humankind;
grace is poured upon your lips;
You, who are closer than our
own breath,
we shall bless You forever.
Put on the voice of authority,

O Beloved,
in your glory and grandeur!

With mercy and strength go forth
for the cause of Truth to
teach Love's way;
with resolute authority lead
your people toward wholeness!
Your ways are narrow, and few there are
who chose to follow;
many stumble and fall
along the Way.

Your Divine Presence endures forever
and ever.
Your sovereign edict is ordained
with justice;
your love is unconditional,
without reserve.
Therefore, O Creator, O Heart of Love,
anoint us with
the oil of gladness to share
with all;
your raiment is as fragrant
blossoms,
healing herbs of kindness.
From every direction stringed instruments
will gladden our hearts;
our friends will be filled
with integrity,
standing beside us in times of need.

Hear, O peoples, consider, and
incline your ear;

forget what has gone before you;
    turn your feet to the path of Love.
Open your hearts to the Beloved,
    learn of humility, be blessed
        in brokenness,
For these are the treasures stored
    in eternity.

All glorious is the soul within,
        the abode of the Merciful One;
    through many trials and suffering
        do you come to the Beloved,
    refined by fire as you follow
        Love's way.
With joy and gladness you are led along,
    as you awaken to the Heart
        of your heart.

Instead of a house of fear, you
        will come to dwell with Love,
    you will radiate the light of truth
        to all the earth.
There will you celebrate the Beloved
        for generations to come,
    the people will praise Love's way
        for ever and ever.

Psalm 46

The Beloved is our refuge and our strength,
  a loving Presence in times of trouble.
Therefore we will not fear though
      the earth should change,
    though the mountains shake in the
      heart of the sea;
Though its waters roar and foam,
    though the mountains tremble
      with its tumult.

There is a river whose streams
      make glad the Holy City,
    the holy habitation of the Most High.
The Beloved is in the midst of it,
    it shall not be moved;
  Our loving Creator is an
    ever-present help.
The nations may be at war,
      countries left in ruins,
    yet is the Voice of the Almighty
      heard,
  melting hearts of stone.
The Beloved is with us,
    the infinite Heart of Love.

Come, behold the works of the Beloved,
    how love does reign even in
      humanity's desolation.
For the Beloved makes wars to cease,
    breaking through the barriers of fear,
    shattering the greedy and oppressors,
      refining hearts of iron!

"Be still and know that I am Love.
        I am exalted among the nations,
        I am exalted in the earth!"
The One who knows all hearts
            is with us;
The Beloved is our refuge and our strength.

Psalm 47

Clap your hands, all peoples!
Acclaim the Creator with loud songs
            of joy!
For the Beloved of our hearts
            is mighty,
        the Most High over all the
        earth.
Love invites the people to
        co-creation,
        the nations to peace.
Love is our birthright,
            our heritage,
        to be shared with all.

Let Love rise up to shouts
            of acclamation;
        join in the cosmic celebration!

Sing praises to the Creator,
      sing praises!
   Sing praises to the Beloved,
      sing praises!
For Love has created the universe,
     let us dance to the flute
       and the harp.
Love reigns over the nations,
     awaiting an answer to its call.
May the leaders of the nations gather
     to bring peace and justice
       to all.
For the earth belongs to Love,
     Who yearns to see creation healed!
      Sing praises to the Beloved!

Psalm 48

Great is the Beloved and greatly
      to be praised
     in the abode of the Most High!
The holy mountain, beautiful
      in elevation,
     is the joy of all the earth,
Clear as a crystal within its
      pearly gates,
Within the stronghold of open hearts
     the Beloved's voice can be heard.

For lo, the inner fears assembled,
    they came forth together.
As soon as they saw the Beloved,
    they were in panic, they took
        to flight;
Trembling before the eyes of Love,
    they labored for a stronghold.
Yet, as in the beginning, the Word
        was heard,
The refining fire of Divine Mercy
    melted hearts held in bondage
        by fear,
In the abode of the Most High,
    where the Beloved lives forever.

We have pondered your steadfast
        love, O Beloved,
    in the midst of our hearts,
        your holy temple.
We call on your Name, O Holy One,
    and praise You to the ends
        of the earth.
Your Word is our armor of strength
    let us rejoice and be glad!
Let all peoples rejoice because
        of your steadfast love!
See with your heart's eye
        the crystal mountain,
    note the clarity and purity within;
Consider well the essence of love,
    the echoes of mercy and justice,
That you may tell the generations

to come
that this is the Beloved,
our hope for ever and ever.
Yea, the Blessed One will be with us
for ever.

Psalm 49

Hear this, all peoples!
Give ear, all inhabitants of the
earth,
both low and high,
rich and poor together!
My mouth shall speak wisdom!
the meditation of my heart
shall be understanding.
I will incline my ear to the Word;
I will solve my problems
through the whispers
of the Heart's voice.

Why should I give up in times of
trouble,
when the stubbornness of my fears
surround me,
Fears that give birth to greed
and lead to exploitation?

Truly I cannot save myself,
or offer a haven of peace to
another,
When my home is like a hornet's nest,
a hive of restless fears.
Turning to you, O Guiding Spirit,
is my strength and support,
a stronghold in times of trouble.

Yes, even the wise are not immune
to fear;
yet, unlike the ignorant, the wise
face their fears with resolve.
Not running away, nor projecting them
onto others,
They trace them to the source,
rooting them out as weeds
from a rose garden.
Thus, they do not trust in the riches
of the world,
but in the Treasure hidden
in the heart.

Others are arrogant in their ignorance,
proud of their own counsel.
Like sheep led to slaughter,
their fears compel them to
walk in darkness,
Guiding them onto unholy paths,
into webs of intrigue,
where despair and destruction
make their home.
Yet does the Spirit of Truth abide within,
veiled by bulwarks of pain.

Be not afraid to discover the Treasure
              within,
        to seek the gold hidden in
              the garden of your heart.
For inasmuch as you root out
              each fear,
        will truth and peace and joy
              become your riches.
You will live in the realm of Love
              becoming a light,
        a beneficial presence in the world.
Future generations will be blessed,
        the bonds of ignorance
              broken forever.
O Spirit of Truth, You are our strength
              and our guiding light,
Leading us to the eternal Treasure,
        the Heart of our heart.

Psalm 50

The Beloved, through the energy of Love,
              brought forth the world.
From the rising to the setting sun,
        Love radiates out to all the nations
              perfect in beauty.
The Beloved has come and will not
              keep silence;
        for Divine Love is a consuming Fire,
        calling forth heaven and earth
              to the judgment of all peoples:

"Gather around, my loyal friends,
        all who by repentance and recompense
        follow the Inner Way."
The universe forever proclaims justice,
And, the Beloved's Indwelling Presence
        guides those who hear with
            their hearts.

"Listen, all people, and I shall speak;
        I will bear witness against you,
            O nations:
As Divine Presence, Eternal Flame of Love,
Shall I not find fault with what
            you call holy,
        these offerings of greed and war
            that are before Me always?
Your lies and deceitful ways,
        your greed for power and wealth
            are spawned by darkness;
Have you forgotten that we are to be
            One in Love and Truth,
        that all of life is Sacred Gift?
I know every creature, every plant,
        every mineral;
I know you—your every need
        and your fears;
The Earth and all that is in it
        belongs to the Whole, to be
        tended by all in co-operation
            with Love.
    Shall I accept your proud and
            boasting hearts,
        the oppression, the injustices
            brought about

through your fearful deeds?
Never shall I accept such burnt offerings!
Rather, offer to the Beloved a gift
            of thanksgiving
        with grateful hearts;
For what other return can you make
        for all that Love offers to you?
My friends, search for the still voice
        that dwells in the Silence.
If you call upon Me in times of trouble,
I am ever present to you.
        You will know Me in your hearts,
        As you honor my love for you.
To you, whose hearts have turned
            to stone, I say:
What right have you to mouth empty prayers,
        and make so free with words
            attributed to Love—
You, who hate correction and turn away
        when you hear my Voice speaking
            within your heart?
You rob the poor with your greed
            and prejudice;
You consort with murder and destruction;
You blame others for your own
            deceitful ways,
        thinking I am blind to your
            iniquities.
The air, the earth, and the seas
        have become foul with the pollution
            of your self-seeking ways
        in the name of nationalism, security,
            and progress.
All this you have done, and shall

I keep silence?
You think that I am another like yourself,
        but, point by point, I shall
                rebuke you to your face.
Think well on this, you who disdain
                Divine Love;
        for you will reap in proportion
                the suffering that you have sown,
        and no one will be able to save you
                from your own destruction."

All who surrender to the love of
                the Great Mystery,
        whose hearts are merciful and kind,
        will go in beauty and walk with grace;
And all who reverence Love's Eternal Flame,
        will know Love's Companioning Presence.

$\mathcal{P}$salm 51

Have mercy on me, O Gracious One,
        according to your steadfast love;
According to your abundant kindness
        forgive me where my thoughts and
                deeds have hurt others.
Lead me in the paths of justice,
        guide my steps on paths of peace!

Teach me, that I may know my weaknesses,
    the shortcomings that bind me,
The unloving ways that separate me,
    that keep me from recognizing
        your life in me;
For, I keep company with fear, and
    dwell in the house of ignorance.
Yet, I was brought forth in love,
    and love is my birthright.

You have placed your truth in the
        inner being;
    therefore, teach me the wisdom
        of the heart.
Forgive all that binds me in fear,
        that I might radiate love;
    cleanse me that your light might
        shine in me.
Fill me with gladness; help me to
    transform weakness into strength.
Look not on my past mistakes
    but on the aspirations
        of my heart.

Create in me a clean heart, O Gracious One,
    and put a new and right spirit
        within me.
Enfold me in the arms of love, and
    fill me with your Holy Spirit.
Restore in me the joy of your saving grace,
    and encourage me with a new spirit.

Then I will teach others your ways,
    and prisoners of fear will return

to You.
Deliver me from the addictions of society,
        most Gracious One,
        O keep me from temptation that
        I may tell of your justice
            and mercy.

O Gracious One, open my lips and
        my mouth shall sing forth
            your praise.
For You do not want sacrifice;
        You delight in our friendship
            with You.
A sacrifice most appropriate is a
            humble spirit;
        a repentant and contrite heart,
            O Merciful One,
        is the gift You most desire.

Let the nations turn from war,
        and encourage one another as
            good neighbors.
O Most Gracious and Compassionate Friend,
        melt our hearts of stone,
        break through the fears that
            lead us into darkness, and
Guide our steps into the way of peace.

Psalm 52

Why do you boast, O proud peoples,
    of your greed against the poor?
    All day long, you plan exploitation.
Lies are on your tongue as
    you turn from the truth.
You love riches more than justice,
    burying your heads in sand
      like the ostrich,
So you are deaf to the cries of
    the oppressed.

Yet justice will prevail in the end;
    your riches will turn to rags,
    you will die separated from Love.
Those who live in truth, will know
    the joy of Love Divine.
They will see the emptiness of those
    who turn from Love,
    who put their trust in
      abundant riches,
    who seek security in wealth.

Blessed are those who are like
      the strong oak
    in the house of the Beloved.
Blessed are those who trust in
    the steadfast love of the Counselor
      for ever and ever.
Gratitude flows from their hearts
    as they walk in truth, as
    they live in unity and peace
      in the presence of Love.

Psalm 53

Those lacking in understanding may say,
    "There is no Divine Presence."
They have not yet opened their hearts
      to the Blessed One,
    to the Beloved, who dwells within.

The Holy Spirit seeks out hearts
    that have been broken,
Ever ready to bless them with
    strength and new life.

Even when a heart remains closed,
    seeking its own will,
The Beloved waits with abiding courtesy
    to hear the inward call.

Many there are who know not Love,
    laboring only for money and power,
Becoming greedy and dissatisfied,
    oppressing the poor and
      the weak.
There they are; fear besets them—
    fear that others will steal their
      wealth,
    that their riches will be scattered
      and lost;
    they live in prisons of their own
      making.

O, that deliverance would come to them!
    For, when they seek the Treasure
      within,

the Beloved will bless them
with joy, integrity, and
eternal life.

Psalm 54

Awaken me, O Mighty One, in your
holy mercy,
that I might be free of fear.
Hear my prayer, O Holy One;
give ear to the words of
my mouth.

For nagging doubts assail me,
bringing loneliness and pain;
I remember not the Beloved, so
overwhelming are my fears.

Yet behold, You are my helper,
the upholder of my life.
With You I have strength to face
my fears,
in your faithfulness help me
to let them go.

With boundless confidence, I
        abandon myself to You;
  I give praise to your name,
      O Beloved,
    with gratitude and joy.
For You deliver me from illusion,
    and, through Love, my heart
    opens to Wisdom.

Psalm 55

Give ear to my prayer, O Beloved,
    and hide not from my
      supplication!
Listen to me, and answer me; for,
    I am overwhelmed by anxiety,
I am tormented by the noise of
    my doubts,
      because of the oppression of
      my illusions.
They keep me bound in a prison,
    and, like bad company,
    they enclose me in darkness.

My heart is in anguish within me,
    thoughts of death keep me
    company.

I spend my hours in fear and
              trembling,
        and despair never leaves me.
I cry out, "O that I had wings
              like a dove!
        I would fly away and be at rest;
Yes, I would flee far from my fears,
        I would lodge in the country,
I would hasten to find a shelter
        from the raging doubts and anger."

Stand with me, O Beloved, clear the
              confusion that dwells within;
        for darkness and conflict dwell
              within my soul.
Day and night fears attack without
              warning;
My heart is weak in the midst of
              this suffering,
        the end seems near at hand.
Oppression and ignorance do not depart
        where truth is a stranger.

It is not a specific doubt that
              taunts me—
        then I could bear it;
It is not a known fear that rises up
              within—
        then I could face it.
No, in my deepest being, I feel that
        You have abandoned me.
We use to hold sweet converse together;
        within the Silence we walked in
              harmony and peace.

Let my prayer be heard, O Comforter.
    Listen to me, and answer me;
    I cry out to You in the midst
        of my pain!

Yes, I call upon the Beloved,
    and Love will heed my cry.
From morning through the evening
    I moan in my loneliness,
    and surrender myself to Love.
The Beloved will deliver my soul
        in safety
    and give me strength to search
        within,
    to find the source of my fear.
Love's presence will make itself
        known to me,
    bringing comfort and stilling
        this disquiet within.
With gentle and tender guidance
    I shall find my way Home.

Fear and doubt sought to capture me,
    weaving webs of confusion,
    breeding lairs of anxiety.
Sowing false seeds of empty promises,
    they sought to take control.
Yet You, O Beloved, were ever near,
    waiting for me to call upon You.

I offered my fears up to the Beloved,
    and Love heard my cry;
I sought the One who ever listens;
    once again, I knew Love's Presence.

Yes, You, O Beloved, bring my fears
        to the fore,
    exposing them to the Light;
I abandon myself into your hands,
Into your Heart I commend my soul,
    in You will I trust.

Psalm 56

Be gracious to me, O Comforter,
        for I dread the power of others;
        all day long my fears oppress me;
I am like a door mat that
            people step upon;
        to oppose another's will seems
            too much for me.
Now, when I am afraid, I shall
            put my trust in You.
In You, whose Word I praise,
        in You I shall find strength.
    What can others do to me?

Too often I succumb to invitations
            not in my best interest;
        I do that which I know can only
            lead to harm.
Others know of my weakness; they
            watch my downfall.

Only with You by my side,
    O Rock,
        will I find courage to choose
        new life.
        In your saving grace, answer
            my prayer, O Comforter!

If You had kept count of my
            transgressions,
        Your tears could fill a lake!
        Are they not in your book?
Now my fears will be turned back,
        in the day when I call.
This I know, that the Beloved
        dwells within.
In You, whose Word I praise,
        in the Holy One, whose Word
        I praise,
In You I shall trust without fear.
        What can others do to me?

My vows to You I must uphold,
        O Beloved;
        I give You thanks; my heart
        overflows with gratitude.
For You deliver me from the depths
        of despair.
        Yes, my fears you help me
        to face;
        they are put to rest,
That I may walk with You,
        O Beloved,
        into the light of a new dawn.

Psalm 57

Be merciful to me, O Beloved!
     I open my heart to You,
        for in You is Love and Wisdom.
In the shadow of your wings I will
            find peace,
        until the fears that bind me
            are transformed.
I cry to the Source of all life,
        to the Eternal One whose Plan
            is wholeness for all.
Send your angels to awaken me,
        put to rest all that keeps me
            in darkness.
The Beloved will send forth steadfast
        Love and Light!

I lie at night in the midst of
            dragons,
        fears that seek to overpower me;
They rise up to taunt me,
        they seek to control my life.

Be exalted, O Holy One, Creator of
        the galaxies!
     Let your glory be over all
        the earth!

My fears have woven a web; like a
        spider
        they seek to entrap me.

They live within me, gnawing at
     my bones,
    they bring only suffering and
     despair.

Yet in my heart I know, Beloved, that
    Love is the healing balm for fear.
I will sing and make melody!
     Awaken, my soul!
Awaken to Love's song!
    I will awaken the dawn!
I will give thanks to You among
     the peoples,
    O Heart of my heart;
I will sing praises to You among
     the nations.
For your steadfast love fills
     the universe, and
    makes a home in my heart!

Be exalted, O Holy One, Creator of
     the galaxies!
    For your Glory reigns over
     all the earth!

Psalm 58

Do the leaders of the nations know
         what is right? Or
      are their hearts set on power
         and fame?
Do they look to the Eternal One,
         the Heart of all hearts?
      In whom do the people put
         their trust?

The ignorant go astray, following
         idol gods of illusion,
      who err in their blindness,
         speaking lies.
They are filled with conceit and
         empty promises.
As the hunter with sweet bait
      lures the deer with intent
         to kill,
The weak become food for the arrogant.

O Beloved, open our eyes;
         break through the darkness of
         our ignorance,
      tear down the walls of our fear!
Let us trust in the Divine Moment,
      living as children with trust
         and joy.
Let us awaken to our birthright,
      free to choose the creative path,
      walking in harmony to the
         planetary song.

Awaken us to the interconnectedness
of all beings,
to all that fly and swim,
to all that walk and crawl
upon the earth!

Those who know Love will rejoice as
the nations learn to cooperate,
as the peoples of earth recover
their true heritage.
People will say, "The time has come
to dwell in peace and integrity;
to walk together in the light
of the most high,
Heart of the Universe!"

Psalm 59

Awaken me from my fears,
O my Beloved,
give me strength to face them
as they rise up within me;
Let your Love envelop me,
and direct my thoughts to
peaceful paths.

Where I have erred in thought and
          spoken in anger,
     where I have acted without love,
          I ask forgiveness.

Rouse Yourself, come to my aid,
          heed my cry!
     For You are the Compassionate One,
          Comforter to all who ask.
You come to those who seek You;
     O Mender of broken hearts,
          create a new heart within me.
I long to sleep at night in peace,
     to awaken to a new dawn.
Too long have my fears, my guilt,
          pursued me,
     whispering lies in my ears
     and evoking beguiling images
          of illusion.

Yes, In You, O my Beloved, I find
          rest;
     You remember not my erring ways,
     Your forgiveness is forever.
O my Strength, I will sing praises
          to You;
     for You are my Rock.
With steadfast love, You stand
          with me;
     You teach me to let go
          of my fears.

Cast them not out, but help me
          face them;
     give me courage to let them go
          one by one,

O Comforter, my Strength!
Let me make amends and start anew;
    let me grow in wisdom and
        understanding.
For the havoc that my fears wield
        within me,
    turns to chaos in my life,
    wounding others and leading to death.

And, as I become free of my fears
        and live in harmony,
    Love will shine through, and
    people will know that You live
        in my heart.
Then at night I will rest in
    the heart of the Beloved,
    my days will be guided
        by Love.
My thoughts will become prayers
    offered from the Silence
        deep within.

And I will sing of your kindness;
    I will sing aloud of your
        steadfast love.
For You have been my Rock
    and my Refuge in the days
        of my distress.
O my Strength, I will sing praises
        to You,
    for You, O Beloved, have
        renewed my life;
    You have set me free to live
        in gratitude and joy!

Psalm 60

O Beloved, why do I believe that
    I can separate myself
        from You,
    as an alien in a foreign land?
    Oh, that I might return to
        your Heart.
You know how I tremble with fear;
    help me to break down the walls,
    to let go of illusions, so that
        I stand tall.
You have allowed me to suffer
        hard things;
    You have not prevented my
        downfall.
You, who are Love, gave me leeway
        to choose,
    to wander far from home.
O my Beloved, be gracious unto me,
    welcome me back into new life,
        hear my prayer!

The Comforter came to me:
    "With joy are you ever at home
        in my Heart,
    as I have always lived in yours.
You are mine; I belong to you;
    the broken are blessed with
        humility,
    the wayward, who turn to walk
        with Love.

Let your mind be guided by truth,
    your heart informed by Mercy;
    then will you know peace and joy."

Who will come to the heart of Love?
    Who will open their hearts and
        know the Beloved?
Who dares to face their fears, to
    break down the prison walls,
        to walk with Love?
O grant us help to answer the call,
    strengthen us with pure resolve!
With the Beloved we shall triumph;
    with Love we shall be free!

Psalm 61

Hear my cry, O Merciful One,
    listen to my prayer;
From the depths of my being
        I call to You,
    for my heart is faint.

Lead me to the Rock that is
        my strength,
        for You alone are my refuge,
        your steadfast love conquers
            my fears.

Let me dwell in your Heart forever!
Oh, to be safe under the shelter
of your wings!
For with mercy, You have heard my
prayers,
You have shown me the heritage
of those who know your love.

Commit my ways to my birthright, that
I might be a co-creator through
all generations!
As I walk on your path forever,
fill me with abiding love
and understanding!

Commit my ways to my birthright, that
I might be a co-creator through
all generations!
As I walk on your path forever,
fill me with abiding love
and understanding!

I shall sing praises and blessings
to your Name, as
I abandon myself into your Heart
day by day!

Psalm 62

For You alone my soul waits in silence;
    from the Beloved comes my salvation.
Enfolding me with strength and steadfast love,
    my faith shall remain firm.

Yet, how long will fear rule my life,
        holding me in its grip like
            a trembling child,
            a dark and lonely grave?
Fear keeps me from living fully, from
            sharing my gifts;
        it takes pleasure in imprisoning
            my soul.
Fear pretends to comfort, so long
        has it dwelled within me;
    truly, it is my enemy.

For You alone my soul waits in silence;
    my hope is from the Beloved.
Enfolding me with strength and
        steadfast love,
    my faith shall remain firm.
In the Silence rests my freedom and
        my guidance;
You are the Heart of my heart,
    my refuge is in the Silence.

Trust in Love at all times, O people;
        pour out your heart to the Beloved;
        Let Silence be a refuge for you.

Being of low estate is but a sigh,
        being of high estate is misleading;
In the balance, either high or low,
        it is of little consequence—
        they are gone in one breath.
Riches, whether obtained by right
            or through extortion,
        rarely lead to nought but greed—
        set not your heart on them.

Once You have spoken,
        twice have I heard:
Our potential gifts belong to You;
        to You, O Beloved, belongs our
            faithful love.
For You render to us all that
        we offer to You—
            fear begets fear,
            love begets love.
For You alone my soul waits in silence;
        from the Beloved comes my life.

Psalm 63

O Love, You are my Beloved, and
            I long for You,
        my soul thirsts for You;
All that is within me thirsts,

as in a dry and barren land
with no water.
So I have called out to You in
my heart,
sensing your power and glory.
Because your steadfast love is
Life to me,
my lips will praise You.
I would radiate your love as long
as I live,
becoming a blessing to others
in gratitude to You.

My soul feasts as with a
magnificent banquet,
and my mouth praises You with
joyful lips,
When I ponder on your kindness, and
meditate on You throughout
the night;
For You have been my salvation,
and in the shadows of your wings
I sing for joy.
My soul clings to You,
your love upholds me.
The fears that seem to separate me
from You
shall be transformed and
disappear;
As they are faced, each fear
is diminished;
they shall be gone as in a dream
when I awaken.
And my soul shall rejoice in the

Beloved;
You who open your heart to Love
will live in peace and joy!

Psalm 64

O You who hear all hearts, hear
          my plea;
     preserve my life when fears
          beset me,
     when the pangs of jealousy pierce
          like a two-edged sword,
When doubts rise up and leave me
          trembling;
As powerful as arrows they strike
          the heart,
     building armored walls that
          keep Love at bay.
They cling like parasites upon their
          host,
     murmuring secretly in the
          darkness,
     "Who can see us?
     Who can cast us out?
We have hidden ourselves well and
          hold strong."
     For our inward minds and hearts
          are deep!

Yet the Beloved will root them out
     with Love;
    they will be loosened suddenly.
Because of their insecurity, they will
     run and falter; and,
    all who see new life arise
     will wonder.
Then the peoples will be in awe;
    they will tell of all the Beloved
     has done,
    and ponder the power of Love.

Let those who have awakened rejoice
     in the Beloved,
    let them celebrate with glad
     hearts!
Let all who know Love give witness
    to our birthright!

Psalm 65

Praise belongs to You, O Indwelling
    Beloved, and
    to You we commit our lives,
    to You who hear our prayers!

To You we come when we go astray;
When our transgressions fill us
            with guilt,
      You do forgive us.
Blessed are those who draw near
            to You,
      those who dwell in your Heart!
Awaken us to your kindness,
            enter into your Holy Temple,
                  our heart!

Through pain and suffering, your
                  Presence sustains us,
      O Merciful One, our Comforter,
You, the hope of all the earth, and
            of the farthest seas;
Who by your Light created the
            mountains,
      being guided by Love;
You still the roaring of the
            seas,
      the pounding of waves,
      the tumult of the peoples;
So that those who dwell even at
            earth's outer bounds
      recognize and reverence You;
At the rise of each morning, and
      as the sun sets at night,
      the people bow their heads
            in reverent gratitude.

You visited the earth and slaked
            our thirst,
      offering Living Streams of
            water;

You fed the hungry,
and taught of Love's way.
You watered hardened souls,
filled with stone and weeds,
softening them with kindness,
and blessing their growth.
You crowned your years with
abandonment,
inviting all to Eternal Life.
In the desert flowers come forth,
the pastures flourish giving
food to the poor,
the valleys rise up.
May all the peoples dance and sing
together with joy.

Psalm 66

Sing a joyful song to the Beloved
all the earth,
and praise Love's name;
Sing in glorious exultation!
We say to You, "How magnificent are
your ways:
So great is your power that fear and
doubt vanish before You;

All the earth worships You;
>   the people raise their voice,
>   they sing praises to your Name."

Come and see what the Beloved has done;
>   wondrous are the deeds of Love.
Remember when the sea turned to
>   dry land?
There, we did rejoice in the One,
>   who rules by the mighty Spirit
>   of Love forever,
Whose eyes keep watch on the
>   nations—
>   let not those who strive for
>   power exalt themselves.

Bless the Beloved, Heart of our hearts,
>   let the sound of our praises
>   be heard.
You keep us attuned to life and
>   guide our feet on solid ground.
For You, O Love, have tested us;
>   You have tried us as silver is
>   tried.
You have allowed us to fall into
>   the net;
>   You have watched us reap all that
>   we have sown;
>   we went through fire and
>   through water,
Yet You have brought us through our
>   pain and
>   into your dwelling place.

I enter your house with gifts;
I commend my soul into your
keeping;
all that my lips uttered and
my mouth promised when
I was in trouble and pain,
I offer up to You;
I abandon myself into your hands.

Come and hear, all you who reverence
the Most High,
and I shall tell what the Beloved
has done for me.
I cried aloud to the Silent Watcher
of my life;
from my tongue came forth words
of praise.
Had I cherished greed and power,
I would have separated myself
from Love;
the voice of my prayer was heard.

Blessed be the holy Name of the Beloved,
Loving Companion Presence,
who has embraced me, and
renewed my life.

Psalm 67

The Beloved is gracious to us
            and blesses us;
        the Radiant One shines upon us.
O, that Love's Way be followed
            in all the earth,
        Love's saving power among all
            the nations.
May the people rejoice in You;
        may all people sing with gratitude
            to the Beloved!

Let the nations be glad and give
            thanks,
        for You call the people to
            integrity and justice;
        You guide the nations upon
            the earth.
May the people rejoice in You;
        may all people sing with gratitude
            to the Beloved!

The earth yields its harvest;
        the Beloved blesses us.
Yes, the Beloved blesses us;
        let us abandon ourselves into
            the Heart of Love!

Psalm 68

Impregnate us with Love, O Comforter!
  Let our fears be transformed;
  let all that keeps us separated
    and confused flee!
As smoke is blown away, so let our
    fears rise up before You;
  as wax melts before fire,
  let our fears be melted by Love!
    Then will we be released
      from bondage;
  we will exult before the Beloved;
  we will be jubilant with joy!

Sing to the Beloved, the Name above
    all names;
  lift up a song to the Most High;
  exult before the Holy One!

Merciful to the poor and kind to
    the lowly
  is the Comforter, who dwells within.
With compassion are the desolate
    given a home,
  the prisoners set free;
But those who run from Love live
    in a parched land.

O Beloved, reach into the hearts
    of your people,
  enter into the darkness of
    their fears;

As the earth quakes, as floods strike
            without warning,
      let your Presence be near.
As the mountains tremble and volcanoes
            spew forth ash,
      let your Presence be near.
As rain falls in abundance on
            desert floors,
         restore the lands that they
               might flourish,
         that the flocks may roam and graze
               on fertile fields.
In your Mercy, O Beloved,
         You provide for the needy,
               You are with us.

A new dawn is rising;
         great will be the understanding
               of those who know Love;
The darkness of ignorance will
            be overcome!
The nations will be united in
            their diversity,
         living in harmony and with
               integrity—
Like the wings of a dove covered
            with silver,
         its pinions with gold.
Then will fear be no more,
         Love will reign in every heart!

O mighty mountain, mountain of
            the Most High,
         O Crystal City of the

New Jerusalem!
Call your people home, out of the
                rubble of this dark age.
        Who will rise up to the Heart
            of all hearts?
        Who will dwell with the Beloved
            forever?

A mighty throng will awaken,
                millions upon millions,
        to the Beloved who dwells within.
They will hear with the heart's ear,
        with their heart's eye will
                they see.
Even many who knew not Love
        will come into the Light.

Blessed be the Beloved,
        who daily bears us up;
        the Comforter who leads us
            to wholeness.
The Beloved calls us to new life,
        and guides our feet away
                from darkness.

Yes, the Beloved will empower us
                with love,
        as we face the fears within.
Love ever whispers, "I will break
        down the walls of illusion,
        I will shatter the fears
                that bind,
That you may walk in a new dawn,
        that you may dance with

          light hearts
      and spread peace throughout
            the earth."

Then will there be a great celebration,
            O Beloved,
         as the peoples come into the
            Light—
The singers in front, the musicians
            will follow,
         children will join the
            procession:
"Bless the Beloved before the
            peoples,
         the Holy One, the Giver
            of Life!"
All nations will partake in this
            new Life,
         from the East and the West,
         from the North and the South,
            will the peoples come.

Call forth our strength, O Beloved;
         stand by us as we break down
            the fears that bind us.
Because You dwell in our hearts,
         we are strong and live
            with courage.
We shall walk among the beasts
         that dwell among the weeds,
         the doubts that weaken and
            confuse us.
We shall root our fears out of
            the darkness,

with beams of your Love.
Let all within that separates us
                beware,
        as we stretch out our hands
            to the Beloved.

Sing to the Beloved, O nations
                of the earth;
        sing praises to the One
                who is Love,
To the One who gathers the nations
                together, to the Beloved,
        whose voice is heard in the
                Silence.
Ascribe wisdom to the Indwelling Presence,
        who invites us to understanding,
        and calls us to live in peace.
Majestic is Love in our hearts,
        the Beloved, Heart of our heart,
        who gives strength and wisdom
                to the people.
        Blessed be the Beloved!

Psalm 69

Come to my aid, O Beloved!
For my fears threaten to drown me.
I sink in the mire of confusion,
    where there is no foothold;
I have entered deep waters,
    and the flood sweeps over me.
I am exhausted from weeping;
    I thirst as in a desert.
I no longer see the path while
    waiting for your return.

More in number than the hairs
      of my head
    are the fears that I carry;
So mighty are they, the walls that
      I built
    can no longer withstand them.
What must I do, O Merciful One,
    to be at peace once again?
O, Life of my life, You know my pretenses,
    the wrongs I have done are not
      hidden from You.

Let those who search for You
    not use me as a guide,
      O Heart of all hearts;
Let those who seek to do your Will
    abandon themselves into your
      keeping, O Loving Counselor.
For in turning from You have I borne
    the consequences, so

that doubt and loneliness now
companion me.
I have become as a stranger in my
own home,
an alien to my inner being.

O, that zeal for your Word might
consume me,
that persecutions assailing me
might be for your sake.
Let me humble my soul with mind-
fasting;
O Beloved, create within me a
clean heart!
Let me live simply, sharing what I have
with those in need,
that the abundance of your creation
might be reflected!
Let me speak out of the Silence,
that through the words given,
others will praise your Name!

Come to my aid, Gentle Healer, for
my prayer is to You.
In your perfect timing, Beloved,
in the abundance of your Love,
answer my cry.
With your strength, O Rock, lift me up,
let me not sink in the mire;
Let me be delivered from my fears
as from deep waters.
Let not the flood sweep over me,
or the deep swallow me up, or
the abyss overwhelm me.

Answer me, O Beloved, for I know of
　　　　　your compassion;
　　　in your abundant mercy, turn
　　　　　toward me.
Do not hide yourself from your
　　　　　wayward child.
Draw near to me as in days gone by,
　　　　　redeem me,
　　　set me free from my fears as
　　　I repent of my erring ways.

For You know how I have strayed,
　　　　　You know my guilt and my regret;
　　　　　my fears also are known to You.
How small I feel when I turn to You.
You who were insulted and spit upon,
　　　whose Heart was pierced with
　　　　　　no one to comfort You.
They gave You no food of understanding,
　　　and for your thirst, they gave
　　　　　　You vinegar to drink.

Let me come once again to your Table,
　　　　　Beloved,
　　　forgive all that separates me
　　　　　from You,
　　　that I might be made whole.
Let me see with the heart's eye;
　　　let me hear through the heart's ear.
Give me the sensitivity to hear
　　　　　your Word,
　　　and the courage to speak it.
May my home become a house of prayer,
　　　that others might come to bask

in your Presence.
May those who have been oppressed
and persecuted
come and find safety and solace
within its doors.

Increase my faith as You draw near,
Loving Companion Presence.
May many come to know You within
their hearts!
Surprise them with the Spirit of Joy,
that they might be glad and
rejoice!

Take heed of my afflications and pain;
let your saving grace, O Beloved,
set me on high!

I will praise your Name with song;
I will magnify You with
thanksgiving.
For I know this pleases You more
than complaints, or
false promises made under duress.
Let the oppressed see and be glad;
you who seek the Beloved,
let your hearts be renewed.
For the Heart of all hearts hears
those in need,
and pours out Compassion to
those in bondage.

Let heaven and earth praise the Creator,
the seas and all that dwell
therein.

For in the Most High lies our salvation,
    the healing of the nations;
And we, the people of the Eternal One,
        are invited, we are called,
    to co-creation, to co-operation;
    thus will future generations inherit
        the planet renewed,
    and those who live the way of Love
        shall dwell with Love forever.
        Amen.

Psalm 70

You take delight, O Radiant One,
    in gracing me with new life!
O Beloved, come and renew me!
Let me face my weaknesses and all
        that confuses me,
    that keeps me from joy!
I seek forgiveness for my
        wrongdoings,
    I desire only You!
Let me begin anew, as a child
        at its mother's breast,
    who basks in love.

May all who seek You
      rejoice and be glad!
May all who surrender to You
        say evermore,
        "My joy is in the Beloved!"
Yet I am lowly and fear-filled;
      hasten to me, Beloved!
You are my strength and my joy;
       O Beloved, come and renew me!

Psalm 71

In You, O my Beloved, do I
       take refuge;
Let me never feel separated
       from You!
In your compassion come and
       refresh me;
     listen to my cry,
     answer my plea!
Be to me a rock, a tower
       of strength,
     a strong arm to uphold me,
     as I abandon myself into
       your hands.

Be a very Presence to me as
       fear grips me,

as I grow old and my friends
leave me.
For You, O Friend, are my hope,
my strength, since I was
but a child.
Upon You have I trusted from
my birth,
You, whom I knew before
my mother's womb.
I continually sing praises to You!

I have been a burden to many;
in You alone will I trust.
I am filled with gratitude and
sing your praises all the day.
Do not abandon me in my old age;
desert me not when my strength
is spent, or
when my mind plays tricks
with me.
For fears rise up to confuse me,
doubts and forgetfulness
band together,
And say, "the Beloved no longer
dwells with you;
there is no one to stand by you."

O Friend, be not far from me;
O Beloved, come and enfold me
in your Presence!
Help me to release my fears.
Hear my prayer that they be
transformed,
O You, who are my Counselor.

As I surrender myself into your
             hands,
       I praise You more and more.
I tell others of your goodness,
       of your compassion and grace
             all the day;
       for your glory is beyond my
             understanding.
As I grow in inner peace and
             serenity,
       I sing songs of praise,
             to You, my Friend!

You who have done wondrous things,
       O Beloved, who is like You?
You who have seen me through
             many fears,
       strengthen me again;
From the depths of despair
       You renew my spirit,
You increase my trust, and You
       comfort me.

I praise you in the Silence
       of my heart,
       for your steadfast Love,
             O my Beloved;
I offer prayers of gratitude,
       O Holy One of the universe.
My heart leaps for joy, as
       I whisper to You in
             the night—
       my soul also, which You
             renew within me.

And I tell my friends as well as
            strangers
        of your abounding grace and
            kindness.
For my fears have diminished,
        my strength has returned;
            I will live my remaining years
                in peace.
Blessed be the Beloved, who dwells
        in all hearts!

Psalm 72

Bring justice to the peoples,
            O Beloved,
        and your mercy to all
            generations!
May the people be known for
            mercy,
        rendering justice to the poor!
Let their spirits soar as the eagle
        let joy abide in every heart!
May You heed the cry of the poor—
            the young and the old,
        setting free all those in need,
        melting the hearts of oppressors!

May we know You as long as the sun
                    endures,
        and as long as the moon,
        throughout all generations!
May we acknowledge You in the rain
                    falling on the fields,
        like showers that water the earth!
In our day may justice flourish,
                    and peace abound,
        throughout all the nations!

May every heart open to your love
                    from sea to sea,
        from the River of Life out
            to the universe!
May fears that imprison the people
                be brought to the Light,
        and rise from the depths!
May the leaders of nations from
            all the earth,
        listen to your Word;
May they spend time in Silence
            before they counsel!
May the leaders surrender to
                your love, and
        the nations serve the Most High!
For You heed the needy when
                they call,
        the poor and those who have
            no friend.
You have compassion on the weak,
                the downtrodden,
        and give them strength and
            hope.
From injustice and oppression,

You redeem their life;
and precious are they in
your Heart.

Long may You live in our hearts,
may praises be sung to You!
May our prayers rise up before You
and blessings of love be
freely rendered!
May we be ever grateful for the
grain of the fields,
for the fruits of the vine
to be shared with all;
And may the people blossom forth
in the cities,
like flowers in the meadow!
May your Name live on forever,
your Love endure as long as
the sun!
May the people bless themselves
by You, and
all nations call You blessed!

Blessed be the Beloved, the One
who dwells in open hearts,
who guides us along the way.
Blessed be You, who come in
Name of Love;
may your glory fill the earth!
Amen and Amen!

Psalm 73

Truly the Beloved is near to those
                with open hearts,
          to those who abandon themselves
                to Love.
But as for me, I almost lost
                the way, when
          my heart was consumed with
                my own desires.
For I was arrogant and yearned
                for wealth,
          when I saw the power of
                the rich.

For they seem to have little
                conscience,
          and are appointed well in
                all things.
They can buy their way out of
                trouble,
          and lack for nothing that
                power can buy.
Therefore pride is their necklace;
          violence covers them as a
                garment.
They become puffed up and
                deceitful,
          their heart's ear closed to
                Love's voice.
They speak with contempt for the
                poor, and
          haughtily they threaten
                oppression.

They rationalize their greed
        believing themselves above
            Love's way.

In turn the people praise them,
        and yearn to follow on
            their path.
And they say, "Because we are
                prosperous,
            we are blessed by the
                Most High;
            surely upright are our ways."
Behold, these are the ignorant;
        always at ease, they increase
            in riches.
Has it been in vain that
        I have opened my heart,
        and washed my hands
            in innocence?
For trouble seems to follow me,
        as I weep over the injustice
        that seems to blanket the world.

If I had pursued their ways,
        I would have been untrue to
            my birthright.
Yet when I tried to understand this,
        it seemed beyond my
                comprehension,
Until I sat in the Silence and
                prayed;
            then a veil lifted and
                I could see.

Truly they walk a dangerous road
        with fear as their constant
            companion.
For when their wealth is lost,
        or disaster threatens to bring
            them down,
They will have forgotten the only
            Treasure,
        they will be so far from their
            true Estate.

When my soul was embittered,
        when I was arrogant at heart,
I was blind and ignorant;
        I was like a spoiled child
            to its parents.
Still You were ever near to me,
        You waited for me to see.
Now You guide me with your
            counsel,
        You hold me in your Heart.
What is my Treasure but your
            love?
        There is nothing upon earth
        that I desire besides You.
My body and my mind may fail,
        but You are the strength of
            my heart
        and my joy forever.

Those who are far from You will
            live in fear;
        You do not compel them to
        open their hearts.

As for me, I delight in walking
        with the Beloved;
    I invited the Friend into
        my heart,
    that I might live with Love.

Psalm 74

O Beloved of my heart, what does it mean
        that I feel separated from You?
        How is it that I fear your anger
            and condemnation?
I have known your Presence in days
            gone by,
        when You counseled me as a guide
            and a friend.
I remember your holy temple,
        my heart.
In your mercy, direct me once again
        before fear destroys me and
            leads me too far astray!

Doubt and anxiety have crept into the
            inner tabernacle,
        erecting walls as a defense.
My mind dwells on hurts of the past
        and foresees a dim future.
All the beauty and joy of companioning

with You
Is lost in the anger that consumes me;
        I become a prisoner in my
                own being.
I say to myself, "I will subdue these
                fears," even knowing that
        only your refining Fire will
                rout them out.

I do not know my inner self;
        how long must I walk alone?
        Like many, will I fear crying out
                to the One, who knows all hearts?
How long, O Beloved, will fear laugh
        at my folly?
        Will it keep me bound forever?
In your mercy, direct me once again,
        before fear destroys me and
                leads me too far astray!

You have companioned us forever,
        working salvation in the midst
                of our humanity.
You fashion us together even as
        we seek to destroy one another;
        You are our Rock as we face
                the demons within.
You forgive us when we are
                contrite, and
        nourish our souls in the
                wilderness.
You are the Living Water assuaging
                our thirst,
        a comfort in our desert days,
                our barren ways.

Who is like You?
Yours is the day, yours also the
night;
All suns and galaxies are established
by your Word.
You created the boundaries of the
world;
the seasons belong to You.

When I call upon You, O Beloved,
pride and arrogance flee,
and your strength upholds me.
You revive my spirit, and I live
in peace; for
You are with the poor in spirit
forever.

I shall always remember your covenant,
as the shadows within rise up
to the Light.
Love will stand by as these fears
are released;
in the Silence where we meet,
I shall praise your Name!

Come, O Beloved, counsel me with love;
In your mercy, direct me once again
before fear destroys me and
leads me too far astray!
O Companioning Presence, make your home
in my heart.

Psalm 75

We give thanks to You, O Beloved,
       we give thanks;
We call upon your Name and
      recount the ways of Love.

At the set time which I appoint,
      I will judge with equity.
When the earth totters, and
         all its inhabitants,
      it is I who keep steady
       its axis.
I say to the powerful,
      "Lead with justice and mercy."
       And to the greedy,
      "Share your abundance with
       those in need.
Let no one see your acts of mercy,
      or know your works of
       charity."

For not from the four directions,
      nor from the heights or the
        depths comes lifting up;
Rather, it is the Most High who
        fulfills judgment,
      sifting as a Thresher,
      burning as a refining Fire.
For hidden within the heart of
       each soul,
      there dwells the Divine Guest,
      that knows well our secret

thoughts,
that weighs us in the balance.

Let us rejoice and be glad!
Let us sing praises to the
Beloved!
As the unjust and oppressors dwell
in the wilderness,
those who live with mercy and truth
will soar like the eagle.

Psalm 76

In loving places, O Beloved,
are You known,
your mercy extends to all
the earth.
Your abode has been established
in our soul,
your dwelling place in our heart.
You break down our walls—
our anger, fear, and
doubts.
Glorious are You, more majestic
than the everlasting mountains.
That which is haughty within us
is brought low,

our greed brings us to ruin;
The violence that we harbor
        turns in upon ourselves.
In your loving mercy, O Beloved,
        You raise us up with Love.

For You fill us with wonder!
        You, who know our innermost
                being,
You forgive us and raise us up.
From the depths of our soul
        You call us to love,
                to grow toward harmony
                        and wholeness.
You well up in our hearts with
                the injunction
        to liberate all the oppressed
                of the earth.

Surely our fear-filled hearts will
                one day praise You,
        the gold that comes out of
                the ashes.
Abandon yourself to the Beloved
        with confidence; and
        receive the blessings of Love
        from the Heart of your heart,
From the One who forgives your
        transgressions,
        Who welcomes you home with joy!

Psalm 77

I cry aloud to You, O Friend,
    to the Eternal Listener, that
      I might be heard.
In the day of trouble I seek the
    Beloved;
    in the night my hand is
      stretched out in prayer;
    my soul yearns to be comforted.

I think of the Beloved, and I moan;
    I meditate, and my spirit
      is weak.
You trouble me and I cannot
    find sleep;
    I am so fearful, I cannot
    find sleep;
    I am so fearful, I cannot
    speak.
How well I remember years past,
    when You were a companion
      close by.
I commune with my heart all
    through the night;
    I meditate, my spirit seeking
    its Friend:
"Will You abandon me forever, and
    leave me comfortless in my
      distress?
Where is your steadfast love that
    made my soul to sing?
    Are your promises empty, that
      I feel so alone?

Where is the Comforter to ease
                this emptiness?
        How have I offended You, O Friend,
                that I am so alone?"
And I wonder, "Is it those walls of
                fear and guilt,
        that separate me from the very
                Heart of my heart?"

I call to mind the closeness of
                my Friend;
        yes, I remember the joy of
                the Beloved's presence.
I contemplate in the Silence,
        recalling how You led me
                along the Way;
For your Way, O Beloved, is holy.
        there is no other like You!
You are the One who will bring
                us to wholeness,
        You manifest your Love to all
                who call upon You;
With You the peoples are redeemed,
        the nations brought to peace.

When our fears sense You, O Beloved,
        when our doubts encounter
                your love,
        they are afraid and tremble.
Our eyes pour forth oceans of tears;
        our countenance grows cloudy;
        we hide behind walls of
                resistance.

The power of your love seems
        too much for us;
    your light unveils the secrets
        hidden in our heart;
      Can You wonder that we tremble?
Yet, You stand beside us as we walk
        through our fears,
    the path to wholeness and love,
    though our footsteps are unsure.
You send the Counselor as a guide
    to lead us on the paths of peace,
        of truth, and love.

Psalm 78

Listen well, O peoples of the earth,
    to inner promptings of the Spirit;
Let Silence enter your house that
      you may hear!
For within your heart Love speaks:
    not with words of deceit,
But of spiritual truths to guide you
      upon the paths of peace.
Do not hide this from your children;
    teach of the inward Voice, and
    help all generations to listen
      in the Silence,

That they may know the Beloved and
            be free
        to follow the precepts of Love.

For the Spirit of Truth is written
            upon open hearts, that
        we might share the Divine Plan,
And model to the children Love's way
            as we have been shown;
That each new generation might honor
            Silence,
        the children yet unborn.
Therein lies the hope of the future,
        to live as co-creators with
            the great Creator:
        Not like those who live in
            ignorance,
        too impatient to wait for Love's
            word,
Whose spirits are not faithful to
            the Most High.

Since the birth of consciousness,
            armed with free will,
        many there are who have rebelled
            against the Creator.
They did not keep the great Covenant
        but refused to live according to
            Love's way.
They forgot their purpose and the
            beautiful Plan,
        and all that had been given
            as Gift.
Throughout the ages, the Eternal Lover
        has shown the marvels of creation,
            wonders to behold.

Remember how the sea was divided so
        the people passed through,
        how the waters stood as a wall;
How in the daytime, they were led
                with a cloud,
        and through the night with a
                fiery light.
Recall how the rocks in the wilderness
                cracked open,
        that the people might drink their
                fill as from the deep;
Yes, streams came out of the rock,
        and caused waters to flow down
                like rivers.

Yet did the people close their hearts,
        rebelling against the Most High,
                living in a wilderness.
Over and over, they tested Love
        by demanding that their desires
                be met.
Speaking against Love, they cried,
        "Can the Mighty One not spread
                a feast for us?
The rocks opened so that water
                gushed out
        and streams overflowed.
Can we not also expect bread and meat
        to be provided for us?"

Did they not know how their rebellions
        separated them from the Source
                of all that is?

How often the people lose faith
          on the journey,
     not trusting in the saving power
          of the Most High!
Even so, their complaints were answered
          with compassion;
And the doors to heaven opened
     raining down their sustenance,
          the very grain of heaven.
They ate of the bread of the angels;
     food was sent in abundance.

The East wind blew in the heavens,
     and the South wind was
          called forth;
Out of heaven's abundance came the
          winged birds,
     as many as the sand of the seas;
They fell right in their midst,
     all around their habitation,
And the people ate and were well filled;
     all that they craved was given
          to them.
Yet justice prevailed, retribution
          was made,
     even as their mouths were still
          filled with food.
To restore the balance, the strongest
          among them died,
     the strongest in their midst.

In spite of all this, the people
     continued to separate themselves
          from Love;

their eyes and ears were closed.
So they lived their days in fear,
and their years in terror.
When they fell, they sought the Most High;
they repented and sought help
earnestly.
They remembered then the Rock,
who was their strength,
the Almighty One, their Redeemer.
Flattery poured from their mouths,
lies issued from their tongues.
Their hearts were not filled with love;
they were not true to the covenant.
Still the Most High, being compassionate,
forgave their iniquity and
gave them new life.
How patient was the Eternal Lover,
how blind to their fickle hearts,
Knowing that they believed themselves
to be but flesh,
a wind that passes and comes
not again.
How often the people rebelled against Love
in the wilderness,
grieving the Beloved with their
distance!

How often they tested Love and turned
their backs to the Holy One!
They forgot the power of Love, and
the times that they were saved,
When they were comforted by signs,
and sustained through miracles.

Through all generations the rivers
            have flowed,
      rivers now polluted by greed.
Through famine and floods, the Beloved
            has brought forth new life.
All through the ages, the earth has
                  yielded its bountiful harvest;
         yet, valleys and mountains, forests
                  and fields have been misused.
Yes, greed has become the great
                  destroyer of life,
         taking without offering back,
         consuming the earth with abandon,
         leaving death, disease, and destruction
                  in its wake.
We cannot be spared what we have sown;
Generations to come will suffer from
                  our willful ways;
         their lives will be a mirror to blind
                  and stubborn hearts.
Injustice, oppression, and greed will turn
                  back upon hearts of stone,
         children unborn will reap a harvest
                  of lost dreams.
Even so, the Source of all life remains
                  faithful,
         ever-ready to lead us out of the
                  wilderness,
         to speak to us in the Silence of
                  our hearts.
Yes, You are our hope, our strength, and
                  our comfort;
         our fears will not overwhelm us.
You will guide us to the New Jerusalem,

to the Mountain of Hope, the
        City of Light!
You will be an ever-living Presence
        to those who call upon your Name,
        to all who open their hearts
                to Love.
When, O peoples of the earth, will you
        stop testing and rebelling against
                the Most High?
        When will you live according
                to Love,
And attune yourselves to the music
        of the spheres?
For as you turn back to the Beloved,
        listening for Love's voice within
                your own heart,
        you will live with integrity,
        you will radiate love.
When you call upon the Beloved,
        your prayers will be heard;
        your needs will be met
                abundantly.
The Beloved is a stranger to those
        who choose to walk in darkness,
        to all who are the enemies of Light.
For You, Love of all loves, gift us
                with freedom
        to follow the way of Life, or
        to live in the shadow of death.
Who will awaken our sleeping minds,
        and lift up our hearts to
                the Truth?

Who will rouse us from apathy,
        quicken our spirits that we might
                serve your Plan?
The Beloved awaits our response to
                the new dawn,
        where the people of earth will be
                united in peace,
Where harmony will reign forever in
                the beauty of diversity, and
        all nations will bow before
                the Most High.

Those who choose the way of darkness,
        who follow the road of ignorance,
                become lost;
They know not the joy of abandonment
                to Love's Companioning Presence.
O peoples on Earth, O nations around
                the globe,
        turn back to Love, build anew upon
                strong foundations,
        renew your commitment to the
                Divine Plan!
Listen long in the Silence that the Word
                may be heard,
        that decisions arise from the depths
                of your inner being where
                        wisdom dwells.
For the Spirit of Truth is written upon
                gentle and open hearts,
                not as on stones of old.
With steadfast love, will the Counselor
                guide you; and

to all who abandon themselves to
the Beloved
will the Divine Plan be revealed.
Amen and amen!

Psalm 79

O Merciful Presence, the ignorant seem
unrestrained in the world;
they defile the Holy Temple, your
dwelling place within;
they leave those weaker than themselves
in ruins.
Chaos and destruction follow them, as
they oppress the poor through
deception and greed, and
kill the faith-filled who resist.
Yes, they have poured out their blood
like water throughout the world;
many have disappeared without a trace.
How long will the unjust bring anguish
to the loving, to those
who seek justice and peace?

How long, O Indwelling Presence?
Will your patience last forever?
When will You awaken our long
dormant spirits?

Pour out your Love on every nation,
open the hearts of all people;
We await a new birth of consciousness,
we call upon your Name!
For the ignorant and unloving are laying
waste to the planet.

Forgive us for the misuse and abuse
of your creation;
humble us with your steadfast love,
before the world becomes a barren
waste.
Help us, O Compassionate One, to renew
the face of the earth;
deliver us, and forgive our sins,
that we might know the joy of
co-creation!
Let other nations not cry out,
"Where is their faith?"
Let all who have spilled the blood
of the innocent
repent and make reparation before
the eyes of the world!

Let the cries of the victims of injustice
come before You;
according to your great Power,
break the bonds of oppression!
Let all that has been garnered through
greed
be returned in full measure with
open hands.
Then we your people, those who would
companion with You,

will give thanks to You forever;
    from generation to generation we will
        abandon ourselves into your hands
        with grace-filled, open hearts.

Psalm 80

Eternal Listener, give heed to
        your people,
    You, who are our Guide and our
        Light!
You, who dwell amidst the angels,
    shine forth into the heart of
        all nations!
Enliven your people with compassion
    that peace and justice
        might flourish.

Restore us, O Holy One;
    let your face shine upon us,
        teach us to love!

Gentle Teacher, help us to turn
        to You in prayer,
    fasting from our negative thoughts.
In your steadfast love, You weep
        with our tears,

tears that rise from fear,
doubt, and illusion.
You uphold us when we feel the sting
of pride,
when our anxiety threatens to
paralyze us.

Restore us, O Holy One;
let your face shine upon us,
teach us to love!

You companion us through the wilderness,
through the shadows created by fear.
You plant your Seed into each heart.
You uproot the weeds of our sin,
You cultivate the soil of our
goodness.
Truly, in You, we become like a tiny
acorn,
holding the secret of a mighty oak.
You nourish us with the food of Love,
with streams of Living Water.
Be our strength as we break down walls
that separate and divide;
let not fear pluck away the gifts
we would share.
Roll away the stones that become obstacles
to growth,
to producing a bountiful harvest.

Receive our gratitude, O Heart of
all hearts!
Look upon us and see what
Love can do;

rejoice in the new birth
that You create!
Be glad where your Seed has found
fertile soil.
How much more the return of one
healthy plant
than ten thousand useless weeds!
May those who have borne the fruit
of love
radiate your Spirit into the world!
May we always walk and co-create
with You;
receive the gratitude of our hearts,
as we share in the Great Plan!

Restore us, O Holy One!
Let your face shine upon us,
teach us to love!

Psalm 81

Sing in unison to the Most High,
our strength;
shout for joy and join the
celebration!
Raise a song, sound the great bells,
the flute and the harp.

Blow the trumpet at the new moon,
at the full moon, and on all
the feast days.
Sing in gratitude to the Great Hunter,
to the One who seeks out
all hearts.
Give thanks in the congregations that
the Good News may be heard
throughout the land.

I hear a Voice I have come to know:
"I relieve your shoulder of the
burden;
your spirit is free to create.
In distress when you call, I come
to you;
I answer you in the secret place
of your heart;
I invite you to the grace
of forgiveness.
Hear, O my people, while I caution you!
O, dear friends, if you would but
listen!
Do not make of riches and ambition a
powerful god;
do not become puffed up with pride
and arrogance.
I am your very breath; I have been
with you from the beginning.
Open your heart wide, and
I shall fill it.

Who among you will listen to the voice
of the Beloved?
How many will open their heart?

All you too stubborn to hear,
    who follow your own counsel,
    will know fear and loneliness.
Oh that my people would listen,
    that, as friends, you would
        walk in my ways!
Your fears would soon flee and
    your hearts would overflow.
You, who turn your backs on Love,
    will know only momentary pleasure,
    your reward will soon be spent.
I would satisfy your hunger,
    and, with streams of Living Water,
    you would live in the joy
        of heaven here on earth!"

Psalm 82

O Merciful and Just Watcher, You take your
        place in the divine council;
    in the realm of conscience, You make
        yourself known.
You give due warning to those in power:
    "How long will you rule with
        injustice
    and oppress the poor?
Act with integrity toward the weak and

the unfortunate;
maintain the rights of the afflicted
and the destitute.
Assist the needy and reverence all
people's freedom;
deliver them from the hand of
the oppressor."

Arise! Awaken to the new dawn!
Come into the Light; shed darkness
like skin on the snake!
For the foundations of the cosmos
are shaking with injustice.

I say, "Within you dwells the Beloved,
the Breath of your breath;
Open your heart in the Silence and
know the One in the many."

Arise! Join in the new creation!
Let harmony reign among all
the nations!

Psalm 83

O Great Creator, do not keep silence;
    do not withhold your peace or
        be still, O Giver of Life!
For fear is rampant in the world;
    those who rule by oppression
        rise up with power.
They lay deceptive plans against
    the people;
    they consult together against
        freedom and justice.
Crafty words belie intent as thousands
    reap dire consequence;
    nations go to war and the
        innocent suffer!
Yes, they conspire with one accord;
    against Love they make a
        covenant—
No institution is free from the
    insidious arm of corruption,
    at home and in fields afar.
Who will succor the homeless, the
    orphans, the starving,
    those cast aside by decisions
        based on greed?
Who will speak up on their behalf?
    Let all with faith-filled hearts
        rise up with Love!

Clothe us in the dress of your peace,
    and the stronghold of your mercy,
    that we might bear the power

of Love;
Let us walk in shoes of integrity,
    and don the mantle of truth.
Let us shed the tatters of envy and
    fear,
    the rags of anger and greed,
And say, "We shall seek only
    the Truth,
    which will set us free!"

O Beloved, let all that is unholy
    within us be cleansed,
    erased as chalk from a slate.
As fire consumes the forest,
    as the flame reaches up to the
    heavens,
Let the refining Fire of your Love
    reach into the hidden places
    within open hearts!
Forgive us and let the deep regret
    of our souls
    rise up as contrite offerings.
Let the people seek your Word,
    let the nations turn from
    violence and destruction.
Let them know that You alone,
    You who reign with Love,
    are the Most High over
    all the earth!

Psalm 84

How glorious is your dwelling place,
  O Loving Creator of the universe!
My soul longs, yes, aches for
  the abode of the Beloved;
All that is within me sings for joy
  to the living Heart of Love!

Even as the sparrow finds a home,
  and the swallow a nesting place,
   where its young are raised within
    your majestic creation,
You invite us to dwell within
  your Heart.
Blessed are they whose hearts are filled
  with love,
   who sing praises to You with
    grateful hearts!

Blessed are they who put their strength
  in You,
   who choose to share the joy and
    sorrows of the world.
They do not give way to fear or doubt;
  they are quickened by divine
   light and power;
   they dwell within the peace of
    the Most High.
They go from strength to strength and
  live with integrity.

O Eternal Lover, hear my prayer;
  give ear, O Divine Comforter!

Forgive what is unholy within me;
    cleanse me of all my sins!

For a day within the Heart of Love
    is more to be desired than
        a thousand elsewhere.
I would rather be a servant in your
        dwelling place,
    than live in riches among
        those who know not Love.
For the Beloved is as radiant as the sun,
    as strong as a steel shield,
    and invites each one to come,
        to partake of the Banquet.
Who will accept the goodness of Love?
    Who will seek for spiritual
        treasure?
O Loving Creator of the universe,
    blessed are all who put their
        trust in You!

Psalm 85

O Beloved, how gracious You are
    to your people;
You restore their souls time and
    time again.

You forgive their iniquity when they
wander far from You;
You give them new Life.

Yes, You bless them and raise up
new hope;
You awaken their hearts
to love.

Restore us again, O Spirit of Truth;
burn us with the refining
Fire of Love!
We cannot live separated from You;
cast out the demons of fear,
doubt, and illusion.
Revive us again, we pray, that
your people may rejoice in You!
Have compassion on your people,
O Holy One,
and grant us your salvation.

Listen, O people, in the silent chapel
of your heart; and
the Beloved will speak of
peace to you,
to the hidden saints, to all who
turn their hearts to Love.
Surely new life is at hand for those
who reverence Love;
O, that harmony might dwell
among the nations.

Steadfast love and faithfulness
will meet;

righteousness and peace will
embrace one another.
Wisdom will spring up from the ground
and truth will look down from
the sky.
Yes, the Eternal Giver will grant
what is good,
and the lands will yield
abundantly.
Mercy and compassion are Love's way,
and will guide our footsteps
upon the path of peace.

Psalm 86

Give ear to my cry, Eternal Word,
and answer me,
for I am in need of You.
Awaken new life in me, as I yearn
to do your will;
dispel the ignorance of my ways,
as I put my trust in You.
You are the Beloved; be gracious to me,
Heart of my heart,
for with You would I walk all day.
My soul is uplifted, as I abandon
myself into your hands.

For You are kind and forgiving,
      abounding in steadfast love to all
         who call upon You.
Give ear to my prayer, Compassionate One;
      listen to my heartfelt plea.
In the time of trouble, I dare to
        call upon You,
      for You hear the cry of those
        in need.

No one is like You, O Mighty One,
      all of creation belongs to You.
All the nations are under your authority
        and, one day,
      they will acknowledge and reverence
        You;
      they will give glory to your Name.
For You are great; we are awed by the
        wonders of your world,
      You alone are the Most High.
Teach me your ways, Mighty Counselor,
      that I may walk in truth;
      write my name upon your Heart.
I give You thanks, O Beloved,
        with my whole being;
      Oh, that I might radiate your Light
        for ever!
Great is your steadfast Love toward
        those who call upon You;
      You deliver their souls from
        the depths of despair.

O Beloved, numerous fears rise up
        within me;

like an army they seek to
overwhelm me, and
they would keep me in darkness.
Yet You are merciful and gracious,
ready to forgive and
abounding in steadfast love
and faithfulness.
Be present to me and receive my prayer;
imbue me with strength, and
help me to release each fear.
Pour forth your Light into my soul,
that all that is hidden in
darkness
may come forth into awareness.
For You, O Beloved, are my Redeemer
and my Comforter.

Psalm 87

In the heavenly realm stands the
City of Light;
the Beloved welcomes all who come
to its gate,
all who have surrendered themselves
to Love.
Glories await you within the citadel,
within the City of Light.

Among those who enter are the humble
                and kind,
        those who reflect peace and
                radiate integrity,
        those who have faced darkness
                with Love by their side.
Prepare yourselves for the City of Light
                all you who hear;
        for the Most High reigns there
                in glory.
Your name is written in the holy register;
        when you face the Recorder,
        who will blush for shame, and
        who will join the heavenly chorus?

Those who live by the Spirit of Love
        will know joy and harmony in
        the everlasting Dance of the Cosmos!

Psalm 88

O Beloved, Heart of my heart,
        I call to You for help by day;
        I cry out in the night.
Let my prayer come before You,
        bend your ear to my cry!

For my soul is full of troubles,
    and my life seems like dust.
I have fallen into a pit of
        despair;
    I have no strength and
      I feel powerless,
Like one from whom You have turned,
    like the soil people walk upon.
You alone can comfort me in the
        deep pit,
    in the darkness of fear.
Separation from You is an agony,
    hopelessness threatens to
        overwhelm me.
Through You alone can I pray for
      my enemies,
    for those who ignore my plight.
I am in a prison, chained by fear;
    I am weary of tears.
Every day I call upon You, O Beloved;
    I lift up my hands in supplication.
Will You raise me from this
      living death?
    Will You mend a broken heart?
Let not your steadfast love pass
      me by;
    have mercy on me, O Comforter!
Reach your hand into the darkness of
    my fears,
    by your saving grace, forgive
      my unholy ways.

O Merciful Redeemer, I cry to You;
    each day my prayer comes before
      You.

Let not separation keep me from
            your Heart;
        be my strength as I face the
            darkness inside.
Too long have I let fear control me,
        projecting onto others the demons
            dwelling within.
Let your Love encircle and envelop me;
        in your mercy raise me up.
Let peace become my companion all day
            long; by night
        free me from the bonds of fear.
Let me be reconciled with family and
            friends; and may I know You
        as Loving Companion Presence as
            in days of old.
                Amen.

Psalm 89

I will sing of your steadfast love
            forever, my Beloved;
        with forthright voice I will proclaim
            your goodness to all generations.
For your abiding love rules the universe,
        your faithfulness extends throughout
            the firmament.

Your Covenant from the beginning of time
        encompasses all who choose to walk
            the path of Love;
And to all generations that honor
            your Word,
        will Love make Itself known.

Let the heavens praise your wonders,
            O Loving Creator,
        your faithfulness in the congregation
            of the holy ones!
For who in the universe is comparable
            to You?
        Who among the heavenly beings
            is like You—
You, who are reverenced in the council
            of the holy ones,
        great in wisdom, gentle of heart,
            above all those around You?
O Most High, mighty are You,
        whose Grace is poured forth
            throughout all ages.
You have blessed us with oceans,
            rivers, and lakes,
        to sustain our life on Earth.
Yes, You entrusted the waters into
            our keeping,
        and in our stewardship we failed.
        Forgive us, O Merciful One.
The heavens are yours, the earth also
            belongs to You.
        Yet we befoul the air and rape
            the earth.
        Forgive us, O Merciful One.

The north and the south, You have
created them;
the east and the west as well.
With the might of arms, we shatter
the nations,
and scatter your people.
Forgive us, O Merciful One.
Righteousness and justice are the
foundation of the Cosmos;
steadfast love and faithfulness
go before You.
Blessed are those who know your Love,
who walk in the Light of
your countenance!
Blessed are those who call upon
your Name
and extol truth and justice!
For You are the glory of their strength;
You give wise counsel.
Our very lives belong to You,
O Loving Companion Presence!

You have made yourself known to the
faith-filled;
You set them on the path of peace.
The Gift You sent to bring redemption
invites us to eternal life!
Through the Heart of all hearts,
You opened the way to Life.
Your steadfast Love came among us
giving us strength.
Fear shall not overcome us,
we will not give in to doubt.
For your Love casts out our fear

and gives rise to forgiveness of
            those who would do us wrong.
Yes, your faithfulness and your abiding
            love are with us,
        and in your name we can do
            all good things.
Through You is our consciousness
            lifted up,
        that we might know your Will
            and live it.
In our gratitude we cry out, "You are
            the Beloved,
        the Most High, our very Breath."
Through You we are born anew,
        the Spirit of Truth comes to us.
Your enduring love is with us forever,
        and your Covenant stands firm
            throughout eternity.
We will know You as Loving Companion
            Presence now
        and in the life to come.

"If your children turn their backs
        and follow not Love's way,
If they oppress the weak and
            befriend injustice,
They will separate themselves from
            Love,
        and they will dwell with fear.
Even so, my steadfast Love will await
            their return,
        my faithfulness will remain sure.
My Covenant stands true forever, as
        does the Word that brings life.

You are all invited to holiness,
>to come to the fulness of
>>your birthright.
For Love shall endure forever, and
>Light as the sun before us.
Like the stars, they shall be established
>forever;
>>they shall stand true while the
>>firmament remains."

So often, You seem cast off and
>rejected, as we
>>your people separate ourselves
>>from Love.
We renounce the Covenant made with You;
>we choose the fear-filled way.
We build walls to defend ourselves,
>walls that lead to loneliness.
The world is rampant with violence,
>neighbors striving to outdo one
>>another.
The nations compete for worldly riches,
>oppressing the weak with deceitful
>>promises.
Yes, when we turn our backs on Love,
>we become deaf to the Word
>>longing to be heard.
We live according to the gratification
>of our senses,
>>forgetting the Treasure hidden in
>>the Silence of our hearts.
Be merciful to us, O Holy One, melt
>our hearts of ice
>>before the hour of reckoning
>>comes upon us!

How long, O people of Earth, will you
          hide yourselves from Love?
     How long will your self-centered ways
          keep you fearful and living
               in darkness?
Remember, O friends, the values that
          are eternal;
     for vanity withers the soul as
          a husk of corn dying in autumn.
Who will come to the Banquet, the feast
          of heaven here on Earth?
     Who will abandon themselves into
          the hands of Love?

O Beloved, your steadfast love remains
          sure and faithful,
     Your promises endure forever.
Awaken us, O Holy One! And humble us so
          we are compelled to cry out
               for forgiveness.
     In your mercy, help us to release
          the fears that veil your Light!
For You alone are the Holy One; You alone
          are the Most High.
     Let all who would be free from fear
          commend their lives into
               your Hands.

Blessed are You, O Loving Companion Presence,
          for ever and ever!
               Amen.

Psalm 90

Eternal and Immortal One, You have been
       our refuge in all generations.
Before the mountains were brought forth,
    before You had formed the earth and
      the world, from
      everlasting to everlasting,
    You are the Alpha and the Omega.

When our days on Earth are ended,
    You welcome us home to your Heart,
      to the City of Light,
      where time is eternal
   and days are not numbered.

You gather those who love You as
    friends returning from a long
      journey,
    giving rest to their souls.
You anoint them with the balm of
      understanding,
    healing wounds of the past.

For our days on Earth are a mystery,
    a searching for You,
    a yearning for the great Mystery
      to make itself known.
The years pass and soon the
      Harvest is at hand,
    a time to reap the fruit of
      one's life.
Who has lived with integrity?

Who will reflect the Light?
Who can bear the radiant beams
of Love?

Who have reverenced the Counselor,
and opened their hearts to the
Spirit of Truth?
Teach us, O Beloved, to honor each day
that we may have a heart
of wisdom.

Awaken us, O Holy One! Too long
have we been asleep!
Have mercy on your people!
Help us to wait in Silence listening
for your Word,
Strengthen us with courage to
face the fears within.
O, that we might be converted in
our hearts
and walk together in peace and
harmony!
Let your Word be known to the nations,
your Glory to our children's
children.
Let the grace and gentleness of the
Holy Spirit be upon us,
guiding our feet upon paths
of Love;
Increase the Light within us—
O Beloved, hear our prayer!
Amen.

Psalm 91

Those who dwell in the shelter of
        Infinite Light,
    who abide in the wings of
        Infinite Love,
Will raise their voices in praise:
        "My refuge and my strength;
        In You alone will I trust."
For You deliver me from the webs
        of fear,
        from all that separates and divides;
You protect me as an eagle shields
        its young,
        Your faithfulness is sure, like
        an arrow set upon the mark.
I will not fear the shadows of the night,
        nor the confusion that comes
        by day,
Nor the dreams that awaken me from
        sleep,
        nor the daily changes that
        life brings.

Though a thousand may deride this
        radical trust,
        ten thousand laugh as I seek
        to do your Will,
Yet will I surrender myself to You,
        abandoning myself into your Hands
        without reserve.

For You have sent your angels to
        watch over me,
        to guide me in all my ways.

On their hands, they will bear me up,
      lest I dash my foot against
            a stone.
Though I walk among those who
          roar like the lion,
      or are as stealthy as the adder,
      in your strength will I be saved.

"Because you cleave to Me in love,
         I will deliver you;
      I will protect you, who
          call upon my Name.
When you call to Me, I will answer you;
      I will be with you in times
         of trouble,
      I will rescue you and
         reverence your life.
All through the years, will I dwell
         in your heart,
      as Loving Companion Presence,
         forever."

Psalm 92

It is good to give thanks to You,
      O Beloved,
        to sing praises to your Holy Name,
To affirm your steadfast love
      in the morning,
      and your faithfulness through
      the night,
To the music of the spheres,
      to the melody of the universe!
For You, Heart of my heart, gladden
      my soul,
      as I proclaim with joy the harmony
      and beauty of creation.

How wondrous is your Divine Plan,
      O Beloved,
      Your design, brought forth by Love!
The ignorant cannot perceive,
      those who still sleep cannot
      understand:
Though darkness covers much of
      the land
      and violence seems to flourish,
Love gives birth to dazzling Light,
      and, like a laser,
      it shines through to all that
      is hidden.
Yet, lo, all those who separate
      themselves from Love,
      will be undone by fear.

You delight my spirit and elevate
      my soul;
    You bathe me in the oil of
      kindness.
My eyes behold the radiance of
     creation's glory,
    my ears echo with Love's refrain.

Those who live with integrity are like
     a garden in full bloom,
    whose blossoms beautify the earth.
They are planted in the dwelling place
     of Love,
    their produce nourishes all those
     who pass by.
All through their lives they produce
     bountiful harvests,
    overflowing as a cornucopia of
     the finest fruits,
Magnifying the Loving and Gracious Creator,
    living as sons and daughters
     of the Most High.

Psalm 93

The Almighty reigns adorned in majesty;
    the Creator is robed and girded
        with strength.
Yes, the world is established and
        given into our care;
    our stewardship of the earth reflects
        our love for You,
    You, who are and ever shall be.

The cosmos celebrates your goodness,
        O Beloved,
    the waters lift up their voice,
    the winds speak through their roaring.
Mightier than the thunder of
        many storms,
    mightier than the waves of the sea,
        is the Most High!

That which you ordain is certain;
    holiness befits your house,
    our hearts, your dwelling place,
        O Beloved, for evermore.

Psalm 94

O Heart of Pure Fire, You who
        cleanse and refine us,
          Compassionate One, shine forth!
In your mercy, rise up and
        awaken those who still sleep
          in ignorance!
O Heart of all hearts, break open
        the hearts of your people,
        that we might hear and heed
          your Word!

Too often we spew forth arrogant words,
        we boast with heads held high.
We oppress the weak in our blindness,
        and turn a deaf ear to the cries
          of the poor.
We ignore the lonely and turn aside
        from the stranger,
        too many children go hungry to bed.
And, we think, "This is not our concern;
        let them pray to God for help!"

Understand, O dullest of the people!
        When will the ignorant awaken?
The Beloved who created the ear, hears us!
The Beloved who formed the eye, sees us!
Like the nations, we are accountable
        for our actions.
Where does knowledge come from, but
        the Heart of our heart.
        The Beloved knows our thoughts, and
        is the very Breath of our breath.

Blessed are those who have confessed their
erring ways,
who have asked for forgiveness.
Blessed are those whose burdens have
been lifted,
who are able to respond with love.
For the Beloved walks with them and
speaks to them in the Silence;
With mercy and compassion, they
are held in Love's heart;
all who are at one with Love will
live in peace and harmony.

Who will stand with Love and act
with justice?
Who will speak out to silence
the oppressors?
Had the Beloved not come to my rescue,
my soul would still dwell in
the land of darkness.
When I recognized my wrongdoings,
your steadfast love renewed me,
O Compassionate One.
When the cares of my heart were many,
your consolations comforted my soul.
Those who live separated from Love,
do not know the peace and joy of
walking with You.
They gather together to try those
who walk in peace,
and with worldly power, they
condemn the innocent.
Yet the Beloved is a stronghold,
the Comforter, the refuge
of my soul.

The statutes of Truth are certain;
    and the Awakening, a promise
        to be fulfilled;
    Who will be ready for the
        new dawn?

Psalm 95

O come, let us sing to the Most High,
    Creator of the Cosmos;
    let us make a joyful song to
        the Beloved!
Let us come to the Radiant One with
    thanksgiving,
    with gratitude let us offer our
        psalms of praise!
For the Beloved is Infinite, the
    Breathing Life of all.
The depths of the earth belong to Love;
    the height of the mountains,
        as well.
The sea and all that is in it,
    the dry land and air above
        were created by Love.

O come, let us bow down and give
    thanks,
    let us be humble before the
        Blessed One!

For the Beloved is Supreme, and
      we, blessed to be invited to
          friendship
      as companions along the Way!

O that today we would harken to the
        Beloved's voice!
      Harden not your hearts, as in
        days of old,
      that you be not separated from Love.
Be not like those who hear the Word and
        heed it not,
      thinking to be above the Most High.
For life is but a breath in the
        Eternal Dance,
      a gift to be reverenced with trust,
      an opportunity to grow in spirit
        and truth,
That in passing into new Life, you enter
      into the Heavenly City.

Psalm 96

O sing to the Cosmos a new song;
      sing to the Beloved, all the earth!
Sing to the Creator, and bless the Name
      above all names;

sing praises to the Glorious One
from day to day.
Declare the splendor of the Radiant One
to all nations,
the marvelous works of Love
to all peoples!
For great is the Beloved, and greatly
to be praised;
reverence Love above all else.
For where your thoughts are,
reveals that which you treasure;
seek only the true Treasure.
Truth and integrity live with Love;
strength and beauty dwell
with the Beloved.

Yield to Love, O families of the earth,
yield to Love glory and strength!
Yield to Love and learn of justice;
make of yourselves an offering
and be guided by Love!
Bow down in adoration and holiness;
for worthy is the Beloved to be
praised in all the earth!

The Creator of the Cosmos reigns!
Yes, the world has been created,
gift to all generations;
let truth and justice give birth
to peace and harmony!
Let the heavens be glad, and let
the earth rejoice;
let the seas roar, and all
that fills them;

let the fields exult, and
everything in them!
Then shall the trees of the wood
sing for joy
before the coming of the Beloved,
who reigns in glory!
For through Love will come truth
and justice,
offering all the people gifts
of new Life.

Psalm 97

The Bestower of Life reigns with mercy,
let the earth rejoice!
Let the heavens be glad!
Justice preserves creation, allowing it
to blossom and thrive;
hidden within creation, You are
the Heart of everything.
Fire goes before You, burning away the
chaff and the tares.
Your Light enlightens the world;
there is none to compare
with You.
All of creation is clothed with
your majesty, mirroring
your Love throughout the cosmos.

The heavens proclaim your righteousness;
and the peoples behold your glory.
Those who walk in darkness dwell in the
abode of fear,
zealously following their desire
for power;
they live in the shadows of reality.
Heaven delights and rejoices when
a hardened heart breaks open and
recognizes Love's ever-patient
Presence abiding within.
For You, O Beloved, are most high over
all the earth;
You overlook our wrongdoings and
welcome us home.

You, O Beloved, are known through those who
are true to the Promise,
You are the Light of the saints;
You hide yourself in every soul.
Light dawns for the just, and joy for
the upright of heart.
Rejoice in the Most High, O people of
the Light,
and give thanks to the Radiant One,
the Bestower of Life!

Psalm 98

O sing to the Beloved a new song,
        for Love has done marvelous
                things!
By the strength of your Indwelling
                Presence,
        we, too, are called to do
                great things;
        we are set free through Love's
                forgiveness and truth.
Yes, your steadfast love and faithfulness
        are an ever-present gift
                in our lives.
All the ends of the earth have seen
        the glory of Love's Eternal Flame.

Make a joyful noise to the Beloved
                all the earth;
        break forth into grateful song
                and sing praises!
Yes, sing songs of praise extolling
                Love's way;
        lift up your hearts with
                gratitude and joy!
Let the voices of all people blend
                in harmony,
        in unison let the people
                magnify the Beloved!

Let the sea laugh, and all that
                fills it;
        the world and those who
                dwell in it!

Let the waters clap their hands;
    let the hills ring out with joy
Before the Beloved, who radiates Love
    to all the earth.
For Love reigns over the world
    with truth and justice,
    bringing order and balance to
    all of creation.

Psalm 99

Awaken, O you people! Entrust your
    hearts to Love.
    For the Beloved reigns supreme;
    let all the earth give thanks!
Your unseen Presence is great in
    the land;
    You sit with the leaders of nations.
Let them be silent and guided by
    your Voice!
    Holy are You!
You are mighty and love justice,
    You establish equity;
Out of the Silence, your Word can
    be heard in the land
    inviting the nations to live
    in peace.

Listen, O you people! Open your hearts
to the Beloved,
that Truth may be born anew!

Many who have gone before you followed
the Beloved's Voice,
the unknown saints of all
generations.
They surrendered themselves into
the Beloved's hands,
and walked with confidence.
They were guided through difficult times,
keeping to Love's way,
and trusting in Love's promises.

O Heart of all hearts, You answered
their prayers;
With mercy, You forgave them their
wrongdoings, always
inviting them to new life.
Sing praises to the Beloved, and
aspire to ascend the holy
mountain.
Holy are You, O Giver of Life!

Psalm 100

Sing a joyful noise to the Beloved
    all peoples of the earth!
Serve Love with a glad heart!
    Join hands in the great
        Dance of Life!

Know that the Beloved of your heart
    is the Divine Presence!
Love created us, and we belong to
    the Most High;
We are born to be loving,
    expressions of the Creator's
        Divine Plan.

Open the gates of your heart
    with gratitude
    and enter Love's court
    with praise!
Give thanks to the Beloved,
    bless Love's holy Name!

For Love is of God, and lives
    in your heart forever,
With faith, truth, and joy, now
    and in all that is to come.
        Alleluia! Amen!

Psalm 101

I sing of loyalty and of justice;
    to You, O Beloved, I sing.
I give heed to the Way that
        leads to peace.
      Come, O Blessed One, make your
        home in my heart.

May I walk with integrity
      where'er I go,
May I see You in all creation!

May I be a mirror of your love
    to all that I meet;
May I reflect the freedom of your
      truth, and live
    as a beneficial presence in
      the world.

Forgive me, O Merciful One, if I turn
      from those in need.
Humble me if I become arrogant
      and greedy.
    Embrace me with your Presence.

I accompany those who love You,
    that I may grow in
      wisdom;
I enter into the Silence, into the
      Eternal Light,
    and listen for your Word.
For, no one who oppresses another,

who keeps company with injustice,
    will dwell in the house of Love.
And, no one who prefers darkness
    will live in the glory of Light.

In the morning I offer myself to You
      in prayer,
    by night I surrender to You
      in trust;
O, that I might walk in the Light
      with a grateful heart,
    and radiate peace to the world!

Psalm 102

Hear my prayer, O Merciful One;
    let my cry come to You!
I long to see your face in
      the day of my distress!
Incline your ear to me;
    be quick to answer in the
      day when I call!

For the days pass away like smoke,
    a fire within consumes me.
My heart is broken, the fragments
      scattered to the winds.

I have lost my appetite.
My groanings never cease; day and
        night I call to You.
I lay and wait, expecting vultures
        to devour me,
            dry and barren as the desert
            sands.
I lie awake, like a lone bird on
        the rooftop.
All the day my fears well up,
        threatening to overwhelm me.
Bread turns to ashes in my mouth,
        and tears mingle with my drink.
Because I feel so far from You,
        separated from your Presence,
My days are like an evening shadow;
        I wither away like grass.

Yet You, O Comforter, are ever near,
        your kindness is made known to
            all generations;
You answer the prayers of those
        who cry to You.
Come! Melt every heart;
        the appointed time is nigh.
Those who trust in You find solace
        for their souls;
        tears soon turn to joy.
All who reverence and honor the
        Beloved,
        are nourished and held by Love.
For You, O Healer, invite us to
        wholeness, to be
        co-creators along Love's way.

You hear the cries of the afflicted,
    and answer their prayer.

Let this be recorded for generations
    to come,
    so that a people yet unborn may
    praise the Beloved:
That You come down from the
    Holy Mountain,
    to live in every receptive heart.
You hear the groans of the prisoners,
    liberating those doomed to die.
Let all nations declare the glory
    of your Holy Name,
And gather together in peace to honor
    the Most High.

Though my strength be broken
    in mid-course,
    and my days shortened,
I cry to You, "Would that this cup
    be taken from me,
    You who are everlasting,
Yet, into your Hands will I commend
    my soul."

Of old You laid the foundation
    of the earth
    and the heavens to reflect
    your glory.
Even should they perish, your Love
    will endure,
    and You will raise us up
    to new Life.

Our lives are like the seasons,
      and they pass away;
         yet You remain constant and sure,
         your years have no end.
All generations to come will call
      upon You,
        until all return to your Heart
        in the Holy City.

Psalm 103

Bless the Beloved, O my soul,
      and all that is within me;
        I bless your Holy Name!
Bless the Beloved, O my soul,
      and remember the goodness
      of Love.
You forgive our iniquities,
      You heal our disease,
You save us from the snares
      of fear,
      You crown us with steadfast
      love and mercy,
You satisfy our every need and
      renew our spirit like
      the eagle's.

Through You comes peace and
    justice for all who are
       oppressed.
You make known the pathway of
    truth,
    and guide us on the Way.
You are merciful and gracious,
    slow to anger and abounding in
      steadfast love.
You love us more than we can ask
    or imagine;
    in truth, we belong to You.
For You understand us,
    requiting us not according to our
      ignorance and error.
As far as the heavens are high above
    the earth,
    so great is your loving response
      toward those who are humble;
So far does your enduring strength
    uphold those who face the
      darkness within.
As parents are concerned for their
    children,
    so You come to those
    who reach out in faith.
For our ways are known, our weaknesses
    seen with compassion.

As for humanity, our days are like
    the grass;
    we flourish like a flower of
    the field;
When the wind passes over,
    it is gone,

and that place knows it no more.
Yet the steadfast love of the Beloved
is from everlasting to everlasting
to those who awaken,
and justice to all generations,
To those who remember your Promises,
and follow your Voice.

The Beloved's home is our hearts,
as we discover in the Silence.
Bless the Beloved, O you angels,
you faith-filled ones who hear
the Word,
following the Voice of Love!
Bless the Beloved, all you people,
those who abandon themselves
into Love's hands!
Bless the Beloved, bless all of Creation!
Bless the Beloved, O my soul!

Psalm 104

Bless the Radiant One, O my soul!
O Heart of my heart, You are
so very great!
You are clothed with justice and
mercy,

arrayed in Light as your
        fine attire.
You stretch over the heavens
        like a tent,
        your Radiance covering the
        waters;
You shine through the clouds, and
        ride on the wings of the wind;
The wind, like the Breath of Life,
        carries your Word,
        Fire refines the dross of
        our souls.

You set the earth on its foundations,
        strong and secure.
You covered it with the deep
        like a garment, with
        many waters that life might
        come forth.
At your Word, the waters divided,
        becoming rivers and lakes and
        mighty oceans;
        storms came to ensure the balance
        and to renew the earth.
The mountains rose, the valleys became
        low
        in the places that You did appoint.
You brought harmony to all the earth,
        that life might spring forth
        in abundance.

You created springs to flow into the
        valleys;
        they flow between the hills,

Giving drink to every creature of
        the field,
            quenching their thirst as your
                Living Water quenches ours.
With the air, You have given birds
        their habitation;
            they sing among the branches.
The majesty of Creation is seen
            throughout the land,
        the sounds of Creation mingle
            with the music of the spheres.

Through your Word, grass came forth
            for the cattle,
        and plants for us to cultivate,
That we might have food from the earth,
        and wine, the fruit of the vine,
Oil and healing herbs of many varieties,
        and bread, our daily sustenance.
The trees are watered abundantly and
            with the sun,
        provide the air we breathe.
Every living creature has its home:
        the birds nest in trees, the wild
            goats upon the mountaintop;
        even the rocks provide protection.
You created the moon to mark the
            tides and seasons,
        the sun, that rises and sets
        in beauty.
In the darkness, when night comes,
        the creatures of the forest
        roam the earth.
They eat their fill, each according

to their need;
You provide their food.
When the sun rises, they disappear
from sight
and lie down in their dens.
As your people go forth to their work,
You are there to guide them.

O You, who know all hearts, how
manifold are your works!
In wisdom You have created
them all;
the earth is filled with your
creatures.
We look to the seas, great and wide,
which teem with life innumerable,
helping to maintain the balance.
O, that we might receive your gifts,
taking only what is needed
with grateful hearts.

All of creation looks to You,
to give them food in
due season.
When we are in harmony with You,
the earth provides;
yes, a bountiful harvest to be
shared with all.
When we misuse what You have created
for us,
we blame You for the famine and
destruction that ensues,
and feel alienated from You.
Even so, You continue to send forth

your Spirit, and
the earth, though not without turmoil,
is renewed.

The glory of the Radiant One endures
forever, for
the works of Love are sure.
You are ever-present to us, even as
the earth trembles,
even as the mountains spew forth
ashes and smoke!
I will abandon myself into your hands
as long as I live;
I will sing praise to You
while I have breath.
May my meditations be pleasing to You,
for I rejoice and am glad in You.
May all who feel separated from You
open their hearts to new Life!
Praise the Creator of the Universe!
Bless the Heart of my heart,
O my soul!
Amen.

Psalm 105

O give thanks to the Beloved, and
        open your hearts to Love.
    Awaken! Listen in silence for the
        Voice of the Counselor.
Sing praises with glad voice, and
    give witness to the truth
        with your lives!
Glory in the radiance of the Beloved;
    let the hearts of those who call
        upon You rejoice!
Seek the One who is Life, your strength,
    walk harmoniously in Love's Presence!
Remember that you are not alone, for
    through Love doubt and fear
        are released;
O people of the earth, ever bear
        in mind
    the unity of diversity in the
        Divine Plan!

You are the Promise of our
        wholeness,
    You await our readiness to
        choose Life.
Your covenant of Love stands firm
        through all ages;
    You forgive us when we stray
        far from Home.
Help us to learn to trust You,
    to untangle the webs of illusion
        that we have made.

As we sift through our dreams,
  guide us to the only Dream
    that brings peace—
  knowing we belong to You.
Give us wisdom and courage to release
    all that binds us;
  for, to face what is built on
    illusion is to find new life.

O Divine Presence, as we surrender
    our hearts to You,
  teach us to be worthy of trust.
O, that what we think and speak
    might be in accord with our
      highest aspirations,
That our faces might shine with
    openness,
  reflecting integrity and honesty
    within,
That we would choose to live in peace
    and harmony,
  our decisions made in accordance
    with Love.
Upon the path of trust, O friends,
  we need not judge ourselves
    or others,
For, as we reverence all life,
  the beauty and unity of diversity
    will be seen.

Gentle us, O Compassionate One, that
  we tread the earth lightly
    and with grace,

Spreading peace, goodness, and love,
	without harm to any creature.
For in gentle serenity is strength
			and assurance;
		confusion and suspicion find
			no home here.
In all things may we be grateful,
	our hearts open to joy.
O Mighty Counselor, speak to us
			within our hearts;
		let your Voice be heard.
And as we listen and heed your Word,
	joy will be our song of thanks.
As You lead us into the Silence,
	we become friends with solitude.
With trust in You our lives become
			simple,
		assurance and peace, leaving
			no room for fear.
All that we have is gift from You,
		O Gracious Beloved,
		all that we are is Yours
			as well.
May we come to see that all
		we give to others,
	we give to ourselves and You.

As the earth produces abundant
			harvests,
		when the sun and rain nourish
			the seeds,
So our fruits bless others as
	we grow in trust and love.

Teach us, O Merciful One, to have
        generous hearts,
    offering all we are in the
      name of Love.
As spring and summer follow
       the autumn and winter,
    so our lives have their seasons.
Help us to live in the eternal
       moment,
    awaiting your perfect timing
      in all things.
May we be content to wait in peace,
      until You stir the waters within
       to act;
    may we be patient with ourselves
    and with others.
O that we may have the light of wisdom,
      the steadfastness of faith!
In You alone is our trust, O Holy One,
    in your Word is the truth
      that sets us free.
O that we may open our minds and
      hearts, and
    welcome You into our home,
That we may live each day
      conversing with You,
    O Loving Companion Presence!

As You have led all generations
      through times of turmoil and war,
Guide us now, O Blessed One,
    along the paths of peace.
May the people of all nations
      break the bonds of fear-filled
        oppression;

may they bless one another
with forgiveness.
Blessed be the One who lives
and dwells among us!

Psalm 106

Giver of Life, we praise You!
Bestower of all gifts, we give
You thanks, for
your steadfast love endures
forever!
Who can tell of your generosity in
all generations,
the rich variety of the living
cosmos?
Blessed are they who recognize the
Gift, and
who follow the precepts of your
Word at all times.

Remember us, O Beloved, as we make
the Journey;
help us to live the Mystery,
That we may fulfill our divine destiny,
that we may co-create with You,
that we may glory in your rich
heritage.

Stand by us that we may become poor
            in spirit,
        acknowledging our own weaknesses
            that lead us astray.
Teach us to be patient with ourselves,
        that we might offer the gift
            of patience to others;
O, that we might learn to be calm,
        to persevere with utter trust
        as we face the fears that
            bind us.
We yearn for all that will bring us
            new life,
        we long for your very Presence
            among us;
Comfort us, O Beloved, with the
            tranquility of your Spirit;
        lead us into calm waters.
Yes, the Comforter will nourish
            our souls, and
        gentle us, that we may be pliant
            in Love's hands.
The earth itself will reap the
            blessing of those
        who become beneficent and live
            with integrity.
We listen for your Word, O Giver of
            the Journey, and
        we praise You with grateful hearts!

Breathing Life of all, we hunger for You;
        and we thirst for purity of heart.
Awaken us to all that is holy,
            to the sacred,

that our lives may be a reflection
of You;
For we love You, and in our hearts
we will to do your Will.

Breath of the Merciful, teach us the way
of compassion,
that we may heed the cries
of the poor;
That we may be merciful to those
who live in the bonds of prison,
illness, and loneliness;
And, may we be strong voices in support
of justice;
may we offer forgiveness as
a healing balm.

Your Word is joy to our hearts,
O, Creator of the Dance.
May we become bearers of joy,
we who are invited to share in
the Cosmic Dance!
We pray for the gift of wisdom,
that the motivations of our heart
might be made pure,
That we may recognize the perfect
timing of all things
and know the seasons of
the heart.
May we walk with faith all the days
of our life—
confident in your Divine Presence,
even in times of trouble,
and with assurance for what is
and all that is to be;

May we have faith in the unfolding of
                our lives, and
        radical trust in the universe!
Awaken us to the Oneness of all things,
        to the beauty and truth of Unity.
May we become aware of the interdependence
                of all living things, and
        come to know You in every thing,
                and all things in You.
For as we attune to your Presence
                within us,
        we know not separation, and
        joy becomes our dwelling place.

Quiet us, O Silent Speaker, that
                out of still spaces
        we may hear your Word;
And, as we ponder the immensity of
                your gift to us of life,
        awe and wonder fill our hearts; for
From galaxies and the furthest stars
        to the smallest atom in our heart,
                You are the Flame of Love.
Forgive us, O Holy One, for our
        wanton ways that have laid waste
                to our planet!

May we embrace Creation as a whole,
        and become attuned to all the world;
May we be blessing to the universe, and
        see divinity in the within and
                the without of all things.

O Great Hunter, search our beings,
    awaken our inner eyes and ears;
Come into the Secret Room of our hearts
    and be our Guest.
Help us to understand and embrace the
    fears that bind us,
That we may grow in courage, and
    challenge injustice where'er it
    prevails.
For as we withdraw our projections
    upon others,
    balance and harmony adorn us;
Our peaceful presence becomes blessing
    to the world;
    we become at one with all of
    creation.
Yes, as our hearts are awakened to
    your Presence within us,
    we are led back to the Source
    of all life.

Call us, O Beloved, to spaces of
    solitude, and
    times to befriend the Silence;
That we may ever know, O Divine One,
    that You are with us always,
    we cannot hide from your Love.
For You, in whom we live and have
    our being,
    distinguish not our race or creed;
Male and female are equal in your sight,
    You take pleasure in the richness
    of diversity!

May we learn the bitter lesson of
          judgment—
     'tis but a mirror of ourselves
          we see.
Increase our willingness to risk, Beloved,
     to be open to change and surprises
          by the Spirit,
     to be willing to suffer that our
          souls may grow;
For our souls increase as we let go,
     as we release all that diverts
          and separates us from You.

Gather us together, O Healing Presence,
     forgive us for the destruction we
          wrought among the nations,
That we may live in peace with all
          people
     and bring glory to your Name.

Blessed are You, Creator of all that is,
     we praise You from everlasting to
          everlasting!
With joy and gratitude, let all the
          people say, "Amen!"
     Praises be to You, our Joy!

Psalm 107

We give thanks to You,
    who are the Source of Love;
    whose Light shines forth
        throughout the universe!
Come, awaken our hearts that
    we might do your Work;
For, without You, we can do nothing;
    'tis your Love that loves
        through us.

Gather us in from all the lands,
    from the east and the west,
    from the south and the north.
Let all who are hungry and thirsty,
    whose souls are faint within
        them,
Cry out to the Most Merciful to give
        them succor,
    to nourish them with healing
        love;
For fear cannot live where love
    and gentleness abide.
Enter into the Great Silence,
    where you may hear the voice
        of the Beloved,
Who satisfies the hungry soul,
    and quenches the thirsty with
        streams of Living Water.

Yes, attune yourselves to the small
    still voice within,

stay true to your heart's Center.
For through your inner being is the
             Word of truth heard;
          the resource to break all bonds
             is found there, too.
Has no one ever told you that
          truth is written on the scrolls
             of your heart,
          that the Beloved dwells therein?
O peoples of the Light, awaken to
          the knowledge that lives
             within you!
Come out of the darkness and gloom;
          break through the fears that
             hold you prisoner.
Do you not know your destiny—
          to be a light unto the world,
          a bearer of peace and harmony?
O let your light shine as a very ray
          of the Radiant One's own light!

And know yourself! Let your aim be
          to recognize who you are.
Aspire to live as sons and daughters
             of Divine Love, and
          to enshrine the earth with
             divinity,
To honor all relationships as sacred,
          to live in peace and in balance with
             all living things.
And acknowledge the sacredness of
             every path,
          albeit different from your own;
That you may reverence the Great Mystery

and the wonder of life!
Remember always to offer grateful hearts
in thanksgiving to the One
who lives among us!

O, that you might learn to see
with your heart,
to hear and think with your
heart, as well!
Many there are who boast of their
own deeds,
who are proud of their power
over others.
Where will they be when storms arise,
when earthquakes shatter the
rocks of their hearts?
Only the humble will call to the
Spirit
to help them in times of distress;
The wise wait not for trouble,
but communicate with the Counselor
in all things.
Enter the Holy Temple of your heart,
and learn to still the tumult
of the mind;
For, to be serene even in the midst
of chaos,
is to know the efficacy of
calmness.
Peace dwells in the heart of silence,
compassion and mercy abide
there, as well.
Come, let us give thanks to the
Heart of all hearts,

giving praise for the unlimited
gifts of Love!
Let us pray for the good of all life,
and learn to dance in harmony
with the cosmos!

Who will offer the dance of their
own life,
as a creation of devotion
and beauty?
Only those who have come through
the darkness
and walk now in the Light
Can offer their lives in service
to build the new world,
where justice and freedom
will truly flourish.
Awaken, all you who are yet asleep,
let us plant seeds for the
commingling of heaven
and earth;
For the Energy of Love radiates in
everything, and
receptive hearts are purified
by its Fire.
Blessed are the children of Light,
for they know their home in
the Universal Heart.

Let your heart be clear and simple,
and your soul filled with Light;
Enter the place of gentleness,
the heart-space of the Beloved,
the embodiment of Love!

For we are invited to radiate the
 Divine Presence,
  to be blessing to one another;
Thus do we become the very image
 that we reflect.
Whoever is wise, let them ponder
 these things,
  let all people reflect on the
  gifts of the Beloved.

Psalm 108

My heart is ready, O Beloved,
 my heart is ready!
I sing, and I will sing praises!
 Awaken, my soul!
Awaken, O joy and gratitude!
 I arise to the new dawn!
I give thanks to You, Beloved,
  among the peoples,
  I sing praises to You among
  the nations.
For your steadfast love is great
  through all the world,
  your faithfulness remains
  for all eternity.

Be exalted, O Radiant One, throughout
the universe!
Let your Glory extend to the
ends of the earth!
That your friend may be set free
from fear,
Come to my aid, and answer me!

For You have been our Promise for
all generations:
"Come to Me when your hearts
are heavy,
and I will give you rest.
For as I am in you, so do you
live in Me;
we are One in the Spirit of Love.
Be my messengers of peace;
be bearers of mercy and justice;
let Love triumph over fear."

Who will answer the invitation of Love?
Who will lead others into
the new dawn?
Awaken, O my soul, to the Beloved
within;
O, that I might be a light
in the world!
Grant that I be released from the
darkness within,
for You are my Comforter and
my Guide!
With You I can do all things;
into your Heart I commend
my soul.

Psalm 109

Be not silent, O You whom
        I praise!
Many are the fears that envelop me,
      causing me to act without
          integrity.
I become boastful that others may
         not see me tremble,
      and I speak ill even of my
         friends.
In return, I become alienated from
         those who love me, and
      from You to whom I pray.
Hear my plea, O Compassionate One,
      in your mercy, come to my aid.

You appoint an angel to watch
         over me,
      to protect me as I face
        my fears.
As I meet temptation, You strengthen me;
      my faith and courage increase.
May the day dawn, when I become
        like the eagle,
      and soar to lofty heights!
May I break the fetters of fear and
      welcome peace into my heart!
May I grow in wisdom and abandon
        myself
      to You with radical trust, and
      may I suffer willingly to reach
        maturity of soul!

May I open myself to change,
        to being guided by the Spirit;
        may I risk the unknown and
            live into the Mystery!
Awaken me to the holy, to the divinity
            of all creation;
        O, that I might honor the sacredness
            of all life!
May all the resentment and bitterness
            that live in me
        be transformed by your Love!
Help me to recognize the unmet needs that
        have turned to desire and lust;
        create a clean heart within me!
Let all that has been stored in secret
        come forth into the radiance
            of your Light;
        O, wash away my hidden faults!

For You are kind and merciful,
        ever searching for ready hearts,
        and comforting those who cry
            out to You!
Implant your gifts within my spirit,
        that I might offer them out
            to those in need!
For, I long to do your Will, to
            co-create in joy,
        to become a beneficent presence
            in the world!
Become like a garment wrapped
            around me,
        clothe me in the raiment
            of your love!

Then will I be strong to face
          my fears
     with a love that is firm and
          sure.
For You, O Heart of all hearts,
          are the Thread
     that connects each one of us,
     that defines the interconnectedness
          of all being!
Though I am weak and yet have miles
          to go,
     your steadfast love will lead
          me Home.
Fear yields itself to Love and
     cannot withstand the Light;
Just as one lit candle dispels
          the darkness,
     each ray of love eases the
          pangs of fear.
O, Giver of the Journey, companion me
          along the way;
     then will I recognize your Face
          in each one I meet.

Yes, guide me into wholeness, harmony,
          and balance,
     that I may be a beneficial
          presence.
Let me give witness to your Word,
     that others may grow in
          trust and truth!
O, Great Awakener, open the eyes
          and ears of my heart,
     let my dormant talents be

made known;
For, with jubilation would I enter
              your Presence,
        to love and serve the great Plan!

With loud voice I will extol You,
              O Creator of the Cosmos;
        I will praise You among the
              peoples!
For You are Comfort and Blessing
        to all who call;
        You love us into new Life!

Psalm 110

The Beloved says to all who will
              hear,
        "Come, walk with Me. Let us
              give birth to a new Earth!"

For, the Spirit is the One who makes
              all things new, and ever
        awaits our "yes" to the
              Dance!
Those who offer themselves freely,
        without reserve,

are guided through life's rough
paths.
Light beckons to light; divine dignity
adorns them in holy arrray.
The Promise holds true forever,
to all generations!
"As companions of the Most High,
come! Claim your home in the
Universal Heart!"

You, O Divine Breath, dwell within
our hearts;
with strong love, You assuage
our fears.
You call us to holiness, to justice,
and integrity,
to free those bound by oppression,
to bring light where ignorance
and darkness dwell.
Come! Drink from the streams of
Living Water.
Come! Feast of the Bread of Life.

Psalm 111

Praise the Beloved, O my soul!
I will give thanks to You with
     my whole heart,
   to all who will listen, I will
     tell of your goodness.
Wondrous is Creation, Great Builder;
   I take pleasure in pondering
     your Work.
Full of honor and integrity are
     your teachings;
   those who follow them will
     find new life.
You lift the hearts of those who
     suffer;
   You come to them in their need.
Your steadfast love is food for
     the soul,
   nourishment in times of fear.
You are ever-mindful of your
     covenant,
   a very Presence to the weary
     and afflicted.
Your Word is truth to those with
     ears to hear,
   your precepts are sure;
Written on the hearts of your
     people, they are
   to be lived forever with
     faith-filled love and assurance.
You bring new life to the world;

Yes! life in abundance is your
gift to us.
Holy and glorious is your Name!
Reverence for You, O Holy One, is the
beginning of wisdom;
a good understanding have all
who practice it.
Your Spirit endures for ever!

Psalm 112

Praises be to You, O Gracious One!
Blessed are those who reverence
the Holy One,
who greatly delight in the Word!
For they dwell with Love, and
their children will learn of peace
and justice.
Abundance and wholeness will be
their heritage,
and truth will be their banner.
Light penetrates the darkness for those
who face their fears;
Love stands by them with mercy
and forgiveness.

It goes well for those who are loving
                    and kind,
            who live their days with justice
                    and integrity.
They become co-creators with the
                    Divine One;
            they bless the world with their
                    presence.
In times of trouble, they know not fear;
            their hearts are firm, trusting in
                    your Loving Companion Presence.
Yes, their hearts are steady, they
                    are not afraid,
            even their enemies are blessed
                    by their love.
They are generous and give freely;
            the needy are offered shelter
                    and food;
            justice and mercy make their
                    home there; and
            their righteousness endures
                    forever.
The unloving are witness to this;
            who knows when the seed will
                    find a fertile heart?
            The fruits of those who know Love
                    are blessing to all!

Psalm 113

Sing praises to the Beloved
        of all hearts!
        Sing praises, all you who would
           honor Love,
        sing praises to the Creator of
           the universe!

Bless the Holy One from this time
        forth
        and forever more!
Aspire to know the Unknowable,
        to enter fully into the
           Great Mystery,
        to be fertile ground to the
           Heart-seed of Love.
Aspire to gifts of the Spirit,
        be open to Grace and express
           gratitude!

Who is like the Blessed One,
        the One who is Infinite Love,
           Power, and Intelligence,
Who enters into human hearts
        and brings comfort to those
           in need?
Yes, those who call upon the
        Merciful One,
        are lifted up and blessed with
           new life;
They wear a crown of joy,
        as they recognize their

oneness with Spirit.
Come, all who suffer and are
heavy-laden,
open your hearts to Love!
Sing praises to the Heart of all hearts!

Psalm 114

Come, all you who have wandered
far from the path,
who have separated yourselves
from Love;
A banquet is prepared for you in the
heart's Secret Room.

There you will find the way home;
a welcome ever awaits you!
Even as you acknowledge the times
you have erred,
the forgiveness of the Beloved
will envelop you.

Call upon the Beloved when fear
arises,
when you feel overwhelmed;
The Eternal Listener will heed
your cry;

you will find strength to face
the shadows.

Befriend all that is within you,
discover the Secret Room in
your heart.
Then will abundant blessings enter
your home; and,
you will welcome the Divine Guest
who is ever with you.

Psalm 115

Those who teach illusion are
ignorant
as are those who trust in them.

O, people of the earth, trust in the
Blessed One,
in the Holy One, who is your
salvation!
O, nations of the world, put your
trust in the Blessed One,
in the Holy One, who is your
salvation!
You, who open your hearts to Love,
will find inner peace,

through the Holy One, who is
your salvation!

The Beloved is ever mindful of us,
and blesses us.
Love will bless the peoples;
Love will bless the nations;
The Beloved will bless those who
invite Love within,
who open wide the door.

May you call upon the Holy One,
you and your children!
May you be guided by the Spirit of Truth,
who dwells within your heart!
The heavens declare the glory of
the Creator,
the earth, too, is filled
with wonder, gifts
of Love.
Fear not for your life; for death
belongs to the Great Mystery.
the Beloved has shown us
the way to Eternal Life.
Let us trust the Holy One from this
time forth and forevermore.
Sing praises to the Living Presence
that dwells in all!

Psalm 116

Receive my love, O Beloved, You who hear
  my voice and my supplication.
You incline your ear to me, and
  I will call upon You with trust
  for as long as I live.
When the snares of fear encompass me,
  when the pangs of loneliness
  envelop me,
  I suffer distress and anguish.
Then I call upon You, my Rock:
  "O Beloved, I beseech You,
  come to my aid!"

Gracious are You and just; the
  Heart of all hearts is merciful
  and forgiving.
You preserve the simple; though
  I am humbled, You lift
  me up.
Return, O my soul, to your rest;
  for You, O Loving Companion Presence,
  bestow grace upon grace,
  a balm for my soul.

You raise me up to new life;
  You dry my tears, and
  guide my feet on straight paths.
Now, I walk hand in hand with Love
  in the land of the awakened ones.
I keep my faith, even in times
  of great turmoil;

I invite others to awaken to the joy
of your Presence.

What shall I render to You for all
your goodness to me?
I will drink the chalice of Love
and praise You, who have done
wondrous things;
I will bear witness to You,
O Bread of Life,
in the presence of all the people.
Precious to You are all who live
in Love,
who abandon themselves into
your loving care.
O Beloved, consider me your friend;
I long to co-create with You.
For You have loosed the bonds
of fear in me.
I will offer to You the gift
of gratitude
and acknowledge your Loving
Presence with joy.
I will bear witness to You,
O Giver of Life,
in the presence of all the people,
In the Holy Temple of my heart,
in your midst, O Beloved.
Praises be to You! For You dwell
in all receptive hearts!

Psalm 117

Praise the Most Merciful, all nations!
    Extol the Holy One, all peoples!
For great is the Blessed One's love
    towards us;
    The Beloved's faithfulness
    endures forever.
Praises be to the Heart of all hearts!

Psalm 118

We give thanks to You,
    O Beloved,
    for You are kind;
    your steadfast love endures
    forever!

Let every nation proclaim,
    "Your steadfast love endures
    forever."
Let all the people cry,
    "Your steadfast love endures
    forever."
Let those who reverence You sing,
    "Your steadfast love endures
    forever."

Out of my distress I called upon You;
You answered, setting me
on a new path.
With You beside me, I do not fear.
What can others do to me?
You live within me and answer
my prayer as
I face the fears that
well up from within.
It is better to abandon yourself
to the Beloved
than to trust in yourself alone.
It is better to surrender to Love
than to seek the riches
of the world.

When all my fears surrounded me,
I acknowledged your Presence
within me!
When they surrounded me on every side,
I gave thanks for your Companioning
Presence!
They surrounded me like bees,
they threatened to overwhelm me;
in your strong Presence,
I faced them!
Though they arose like an army,
You stood firm beside me.
You are my strength and my song;
You are my Counselor and my Friend.

Harken to songs of victory,
to the music of my soul;

"You, O Loving Presence, have been
            my strength,
      You have stood beside me
            in the darkness,
      You have walked with me
            into the light!"
I shall not give in to fear,
      but I shall live in peace
      and give witness to your
            saving grace.
You turned your face from my
            weaknesses, and
      You opened the door leading
            to new life.

Yes, You opened to me the gates
            of truth and justice
      that I might enter through them.
      Praise be to You, O Merciful One!

This is the gate to Life;
      those who know Love shall
            enter through it.

I give thanks to You, O Beloved, who
            answer our prayers
      and invite us to new Life.
The stone which the builders rejected
      has become the foundation
            of our lives.
This, O Eternal Listener, is your work;
      it is marvelous in our eyes.
This is the day which You have made;
      let us rejoice and be glad in it!

Remain ever by our side, O Friend!
Come, live in our hearts as
Loving Companion Presence!

Blessed are all who enter through
your gates!
Blessed are all who dwell in
the house of Love!
For You lead the Way, You forgive
our misguided ways, and
You bring Light into darkness.
Come, all you who will, partake of
the Great Banquet!

You are my Beloved, and I will
give thanks to You;
You are my Beloved, greatly
will I praise You!

We give thanks to You, O Blessed One,
for You are kind; your steadfast
love endures for ever!

Psalm 119

Blessed are those whose ways are
        blameless,
    who live with spiritual integrity!
Blessed are those who honor the
        Inner Being,
    who follow You with their
        whole heart,
Who enfold the world with love
    and walk on peaceful paths!
You have shown us the way of Truth,
    the way that leads to freedom.
O, that I might ever reflect the
        Light!
Then I shall know inner peace, as
    I surrender myself into
        your Hands.
I will praise You with a grateful
        heart,
    as I lean on your great
        kindness.
As I forsake the path of darkness,
    O have mercy on me!

How can the young keep to the
        straight path? Only
    by learning to listen to the
        still Voice within.
With all my heart I seek You;
    let me not wander from
        your teachings!
Your Word is imprinted upon my heart,

that I may walk in your Light.
Blessed are You, O Counselor;
    guide me in all that I do,
That with my lips I may bear
    witness to the truth of your Way.
With your Word in my heart,
        I delight more than with the
            world's riches.
I listen in the Silence,
    awaiting the clarity of your
        counsel.
May I become a living fountain of joy
    and give thanks for your
        bountiful blessings!

I give myself into your Hands,
    that I may live fully
        into your Word.
Open my heart's eyes, that I may see
    the wondrous blessings of
        creation.
I am a sojourner on earth;
    may I know myself also as a
        spiritual being!
My soul is consumed with an intense
        longing
    to be blessed and sustained by You,
        O Divine Lover!
May I not be a bearer of disharmony,
    one who is arrogant and greedy;
Teach me to stand firm when faced with
        injustice and oppression,
    to be fervent in my stance
        for truth!

Even though fears rise up,
may my eye remain focused on You.
For in your Word do I delight;
You are my Couselor!

With my heart's ear I hear the
injunction
to pray for my enemies,
even those who persecute me!
How can I, weak and fear-filled,
heed this difficult teaching?
Help me to understand the way of
your precepts, and
give me strength to follow through.
My soul is willing, O Merciful One,
yet the body would flee.
Who is the enemy from whom I run,
but the fears hidden in the
shadows within!
Strengthen me according to your Word,
lead me gently into the Light.
For, I have chosen the way of
faithfulness;
with trust in You, I will face
my own darkness.
I will not run from the fears that
beset me, so that
each one may be transformed in
your Love.

Help me to know, O Teacher, the
path to follow You;
lead the way and I will come.
In your love is the power to calm

the storms of adversity;
show me the power of your
forgiving love.
O that I might learn to bless others
selflessly,
to be a silent benediction!
Incline my heart to your Word,
and not to gain!
Turn my eyes from the world's
temptations, and
birth me into new Life.
Let me enter into the realm where
the aspirations of my soul may
become manifest.
Clothe me with compassion that
I may answer the cries of those
in need.
Do You see how I long to serve
with You?
In your mercy, hear my prayer!

You ever enfold us in the power of
your boundless love,
according to your Promise to us;
You have implanted the Divine Seed
in every heart,
a Treasure beyond words.
Teach us to nurture that Seed so
it might blossom into fulness
and maturity.
O, Giver of Life, may we recognize
the Divine Seed in every person;
May we be sensitive to all we meet
along the way,

blessing and encouraging one
another;
May we know that who we are is
a reflection of You, the
Divine Seed we bear.
You are the Sunlight of our heart,
the Water that brings
forth Life!
Praises be to You, O Holy One
of Ineffable Power!

I meditate on your Word living
in my heart,
that renews and refreshes me.
This is my comfort when doubts arise,
the secret Promise of Life.
Though others do not understand me,
assurance and peace in You
sustain me.
Let my self-made spirit decrease,
that I may be rich in your
Divine Spirit!
Let me carry the crosses that
come to me,
with your strength to bear me up.
May I become hollow like the reed,
so You may play your melody
through me.
For I long to be attuned to the great
song of the Cosmos,
to know the song of inner praise!
O, that I might hear the Divine Melody
within
and give birth to a dancing star!

You are my portion;
    You are the sacred Gift of Life.
Though You speak to the ears of
        every heart, yet
    not every heart will hear You.
O friends, close not the eyes of
        your heart
        to the light of Truth!
Rejoice in the glorious and sacred
        Giver of Life,
    clothe yourself with joy!
Feel your heart expand in gratitude,
    and learn from the earth
        of humility.
I will sing praises to You throughout
        the day, and
    meditate on Love during
        the night.
For You are Companion and Friend
    to all who reverence your ways.
The earth is filled with Divine Love;
    O, that I might know You in
        all things!

You are fulfilling your promises
        in me,
    O Faithful One, according to
        your Word.
Teach me good judgment and
        understanding,
    for I know your teachings
        are sure.
Before, I was sorely afraid and
        I went astray;

but now, I hold to your Word.
You are good, and all good comes
from You;
help me to share the
treasures of the heart.
May I come to live with patience,
waiting for your perfect timing
in all circumstances.
May tolerance make its home in me,
that I recognize You in
every heart.
May I be imbued with goodness, and
make room for kindness in
all situations.
For your ways are far richer
than thousands of gold and
silver pieces.

Your hands and love created and
fashioned me;
give me understanding that
I may live fully in You.
Those who live with fear and in
darkness,
shall see how You have transformed
my life.
They will rejoice and turn away
from empty paths;
they will find hope in your Word.
May I always welcome love and
assurance, and
offer these gifts to those
who weep and live with doubt.

Let your mercy and compassion wash
            over me,
        that I may ever work on behalf
            of justice.
And grant me a generous heart,
            O, my Friend and Teacher,
        for I would give freely of my time
            and energy in your Name.

Let me be a witness to You to
        those who are filled with fear.
Create in me a clean heart,
        that your Light might be seen!

My soul sighs awaiting your
            living Presence; for
        I sense your Love and Light.
My heart wells up with gratitude
            and praise, as
        I recall the innumerable blessings
            You continually bestow.
When I ponder the plight of the world,
        my heart weeps for all the
            oppressed.
How long, O Merciful One, must we
            endure the greed,
        the arrogance of those who are
            in power—
Those whose hearts have turned
            from You,
        who follow not the way
            of Love,

Who have become blind to the Truth,
and deaf to the Word hidden
in their hearts?

Awaken the people of earth, O You,
who are the Great Awakener!
In your steadfast love, melt all hearts
that have turned to stone;
long have we awaited a great
Spirit-quake.

O Holy One, your Word is firmly
fixed in the heavens.
Your faithfulness endures to all
generations;
Love is the hope and promise
of all the Earth.
Help us to reverence Her, to care
for Her with compassion;
for we have sorely misused Her.
If You had withheld your Word
from us,
we would have perished from
our fears.
Your Truth is ever before us;
by it, You have set us free.

I am yours, grace me with your Presence,
for I would be a loving friend
and companion to You.
I say to those I meet, "Come,
the way is yours!
Come, all you who are fearful
and lonely!

Follow the sacred path of Truth;
    Come to the inner way of Light!"

O, how I love your friendship!
    I walk with You wherever I go.
Your love is the life-giving force
        of Creation,
        imbue us with your living rays
        of Love.
For, as we surrender ourselves to
        your living Presence,
    we will be filled with the
        radiance of Love.
As we open our hearts to the spiritual
        life,
    we will be filled with wisdom,
        freedom and joy.
O, how glorious are the ways of the
        Spirit!
    How wondrous are your Works!
The path of love is sure, unhurried
        and filled with mystery.
How sweet are your words to my taste,
    sweeter than honey to my mouth!
Through your Word I receive understanding;
    I no longer take pleasure in my
        former ways.

Yes, your Word is a lamp to my feet
    and a light to my path.
You give me strength as I descend into
        the inner sanctum,
    to uncover the truth hidden there,
    to seek the treasures of the Spirit.

When I am filled with fear,
    I meditate upon your light.
I yearn to have every doubt and fear
       quelled and transformed;
O, Heart of all hearts, bless me with
      your healing light,
    that I may be a loving presence.

Though the ignorant lay snares for me,
    let me not stray from You.
Your Word is my heritage forever;
    yes, it is the joy of my heart.
I shall open my heart's ear to converse
      with You
    forever, to the end.

When I meditate upon your light,
    my heart opens with compassion for
      all life.
This is how the veil is lifted,
    how the soul is filled with
      truth and light.
Then we will not judge others, and
    we will radiate love and healing
      to the world.
For as we develop the capacity to
      bless others,
    we will lighten the fears in
      the world.
Uphold us according to your Promise,
    that we may love;
    let not ignorance find a home
      in us.
Even should we go astray and wander

far from You,
You will ever love us;
We have only to turn back and acknowledge
our regret, and
You forgive us with undying love.
O friends, let us sing praises before
such a Gift,
before such all-enfolding Love,
Wisdom, and Power!

O, that my soul would live from
its innermost being, and
give witness to truth in thought,
word, and deed!
For, only then will I see the glorious
vision
and hear the Voice of the Beloved.
Teach me the way of discernment
that I make choices with integrity.
In your steadfast love, may I know
the joy of responsibility for
all my deeds.
Give me courage for all the trials,
testings, and training as
I choose the spiritual path.

Breathe on me, O Breath of Inspiration,
in the silence of my tranquil heart,
infill me with your wisdom.
O, that I might radiate the compassion
and peace,
the truth and beauty of the Beloved!
Direct my steps, O Holy One, that
I may humbly walk with You.

The witness of your Life is
            my model;
        therefore my soul yearns for You.
The unfolding of your Word gives light;
        it imparts understanding to
            the simple.
My mouth pours forth praise continually,
        for I am ever grateful for
            your Promises.
You come to me and are gracious to me,
        as You are to all who open
            their heart's door.
Guide my steps according to your
            Word,
        and show me how to lovingly
            co-create with You.
Let me not be lured by the
            world's values,
        that I may walk the path of
            wholeness.
May your face shine upon your
            friend, as
        You teach me of Love.
I weep over our wounded world,
        our earth ravaged by greedy,
            insensitive hands.

O friends, you who are fearful
            of Love,
        you, who live in loneliness,
Break open the locks of your
            heart's door,
        breathe deeply of sunlight's
            freedom and warmth.

Wander no longer in the storms of
            ignorance and fear; for
        the bonds of darkness will disappear
        as you enter the new dawn of Light!
Hold tightly to the hand of faith
        for strength through deep valleys;
Learn to trust in the One,
        who is ever your companion
            and guide.

Be not afraid of Love's touch,
        the Fire that consumes all
            dross;
For Love is the great transformer,
        burning away false ways of the
            past, and
        filling the heart with Light.
Awaken to the Indwelling Presence of
        the Beloved!
        Envision the beauty that Love
            brings forth!

When faced with slow progress, and
            seemingly endless delays,
        You enfold me in your patient
            Heart.
Let me recognize your perfect timing
        in all things,
        the fulness of your providence.
May I be so strong in your Spirit
        that all I do is inspired by You.
For You are loving, kind, and gentle;
        in You are all blessings.
Let me not be deaf to your Word,

nor suffer the pain of a
                rebellious soul.
Gentle me, O Loving Guide, that
                I may learn
        the wisdom of purity, meekness,
                and peace.
Teach me of mercy, O You who are
                the Merciful One,
        that my soul may serve with You
                joyfully and with love.
O friends, open your heart to
                the divine life!
        Attune yourself to the Divine Guest
                within your being!

For, when you come to know the
                Source of your life,
        love flows through you and
                radiates outward;
Harmony enters into your life,
        you see with new eyes.
All that once brought pain and
                suffering
        no longer affects the peace in
                your heart.
Through the healing forgiveness
                of Love,
        all past wrongs are righted;
Joy comes alive in your heart,
        the joy of understanding.
Then do you know the great
                Treasure,
        the pearl hidden in the Secret
                Realm within.

Glorious is the life of the soul
    when illumined by the
        Divine Spirit.
Search for it, friends, count not
        the years;
    search in the stillness of
        your innermost being!

Abandon yourself to the Beloved,
    draw closer and closer to Love.
For when you dwell in peace within
        Love's heart,
    and know the Divine Spirit in
        your own heart,
You become as nothing, yet
    all things are yours.
As you radiate the healing love of
        your inmost being
    into a suffering, scarred, yet
        ever-sacred world,
Offer grateful praise from the chalice
        of your heart
    to the One who loves through you.
Great peace have those who co-create
        with You,
    who share the living wine of
        your Spirit.
They know that all goodness comes
        from your Divine Love,
    the Source and Foundation of
        all life.
Fill us, O Gracious One, with your
        loving wisdom,
    guide all hearts on paths
        of peace.

When the journey seems long,
    when we become discouraged
      along the way,
You uphold and sustain us,
    You restore us with your
      saving grace.
When we stumble and stray amid the
      thorns on false paths,
    we are ever humbled by your
      forgiving love.

You welcome us home as honored
      guests,
    back into the fold of your Heart.
You have prepared a garden for us,
    a garden of joy hidden in
      our hearts.
O friends, enter into this eternal
      garden,
    befriend the Guide who
      awaits you.
Enter into the great, resounding Silence,
    be still and know true peace;
Know the all-embracing life of Love;
    and raise your voice with grateful
      acclamations of praise!
      Amen.

Psalm 120

In my distress I cry to You,
    that You may come quickly
        to comfort me:
"Be strong in me, that I might
        face the darkness,
    the despair that rises up
        from the depths."

I am bowed down with remorse:
    for my inappropriate choices,
        forgive me, O Healer.
For all my betrayals of others and
        to my own soul,
    forgive me, O Healer.
Bless my tears that flow like a
        stream running to meet
    the Living Waters of your Love.
Too long have I lived with guilt,
    my shame blinding me to
        your Love.
I yearn to live in peace; come quickly!
    Strengthen me as I face
        the darkness within!

Psalm 121

My heart's eyes behold your
    Divine Glory!
      From whence does my help come?
My help comes from You,
    who created heaven and earth.

You strengthen and uphold me,
    You, who are ever by my side.
Behold! You who watch over the
      nations
    will see all hearts awaken
      to the Light.

For You are the Great Counselor;
    You dwell within all hearts,
    that we might respond to the
      Universal Heart—
Like the sun, that nourishes us by day,
    like the stars that guide the
      wayfarer at night.
In You we shall not be afraid of
    the darkness, for
    You are the Light of our life.
May You keep us in our going out
    and our coming in
    from this time forth and
      forevermore.

Psalm 122

My spirit soared when a Voice
        spoke to me:
          "Come, come to the Heart
            of Love!"
How long I had stood within the
        house of fear
         yearning to enter the gates
          of Love!

The New Jerusalem, the Holy City,
        is bound firmly together;
All who seek the Heart of Love,
        those who have faced their fears,
Enter the gates in peace and with
           great joy,
         singing songs of thanksgiving.
There, in harmony with the cosmos,
        the community gathers united
         in love.

Pray for the peace of the world!
        May all nations prosper as one!
May peace reign among all peoples,
        and integrity dwell within
         every heart!
Then will friends and neighbors, and
         former enemies as well,
        cry out, "Peace be within you!"
For the good of the universe and
        in gratitude to the Beloved,
Let us serve the Holy One
         of all nations
         with glad hearts.

Psalm 123

To You I lift up my spirit,
    You, who are enthroned
        in every heart!
For, as the young child holds tightly
    the hand of its parent,
As those in the throes of disease
    look to one who brings comfort,
So our spirits seek the Heart of love,
    that we might find mercy
        and forgiveness.

Have mercy on us, O Compassionate One,
        have mercy,
    that we might turn from our
        blind and ignorant ways.
Too long our souls have been veiled
        by fear;
    have mercy, lead us to the
        path of wholeness.

Psalm 124

If it were not for You, O Beloved,
      You who make all things new,
Fear and chaos would reign
          in every heart;
      in You will I trust.
When doubt threatens to overwhelm
          and separate me,
      when anger makes me blind,
Then You, O Merciful One, are
          ever-ready
      to awaken the holy, the sacred
      within me;
Then do your Living Streams of Grace
      enfold me.

Blessed are You, who are a very
          Presence to us,
      a comfort to troubled hearts!
Grant us the strength of eagle wings,
      the courage to soar to new heights!
Break within us the bonds of fear
      that we may live with love!

Our guidance comes from You,
      O Counselor,
          Blessed are You, O Giver of Life!
          Beloved of my heart!

Psalm 125

Those who put their trust in You
              are like giant trees
          standing firm and rooted deep.
As the trees grow strong in fertile
              soil,
          so we mature in the garden of
              Love,
          nourished by the Word of Life.
For the weeds of fear, the tares
              of ignorance,
          find no home here; they are
             soon cast out.
As each flower in its uniqueness
              blesses the garden,
          the interconnectedness of all
              brings it to fulfillment.
Those whose lives reflect goodness
              and integrity,
          become mirrors to Love's way.
They are like fragrant blossoms that
          bring joy to all around them,
          like open invitations for others
              to come.
          Come! Enter the Garden of Love!

Psalm 126

When the Divine Lover enters the
　　　　　human heart,
　　　all yearnings are fulfilled!
Then will our mouths ring forth
　　　　　with laughter, and
　　　our tongues with shouts of joy;
Then will we sing our songs of praise,
　　　to You, O Beloved of all hearts.
For gladness will radiate out for
　　　　　all to see;
　　　so great is your Presence
　　　　　among us.

Restore us to wholeness, O Healer,
　　　like newborn babes who have
　　　　　never strayed from You!
May all who sow in tears
　　　reap with shouts of joy!
May all who go forth weeping tears
　　　　　of repentance,
　　　bearing seed for sowing,
Come home to You with shouts
　　　　　of joy,
　　　leaving sorrow behind.

Psalm 127

Unless You, O Divine Creator, build
      the house,
    those who build it labor in vain.
Unless You watch over the city,
    the watchers stay awake in vain.
For it is in co-operating with You
      from morn to evening,
Eating the bread of your Word,
    that we rest in peace throughout
      the night.

Reverence the sacred gift of life that
      nourishes all.
Who will grow in wisdom, abandoning
    themselves into the chalice of Love?
Who will open themselves to the
    imprint of Love's gifts upon
      their heart?
Unless You, O Divine Spirit, make
      your home within us,
    we wander through life in vain.

Psalm 128

Blessed are you who reverence
       the Beloved,
    who walk in Love's way!
You radiate an inner joy
       and peace where'er you go;
    compassion draws you to
       the gates of those in need.

Families and friends gather upon
       your doorstep;
Children run to greet you with
       open arms.
Yes, blessed are you who reverence
    the Beloved!

Strangers feel at home in
       your presence;
    the oppressed are comforted
       by your support.
Blessed indeed are you who reverence
    the Beloved!
      Peace be within you!

Psalm 129

Life up your hearts to the Most High!
Let the earth ring with songs
              of praise!
         Be glad, O people of the
              Light!
Let your life be impregnated by
              Love's gifts.
Discover in the Great Silence the
         mystery of who you are,
         and be true to your self.
For wherever you dwell,
         there is beauty;
         Infinite Love is everywhere.
Know that the beauty hidden within
              your soul,
         is seen by the eyes of
              your heart.
Let the still small voice of
              the Beloved
         guide you by day and
         comfort you at night;
Then will you be blessed and,
              in turn,
         you will be blessing to
              the world.

Psalm 130

Out of the depths I cry to You!
    In your Mercy, hear my voice!
Let your ears be attentive to
    the voice of my supplications!

If You should number the times we
    stray from You, O Beloved,
        who could face You?
Yet You are ever-ready to forgive,
    that we might be healed.

I wait for You, my soul waits,
    and in your Word, I hope;
My soul awaits the Beloved
    as one awaits the birth
        of a child, or
    as one awaits the fulfillment
        of their destiny.

O sons and daughters of the Light,
    welcome the Heart of your heart!
    Then you will climb the Sacred
        Mountain of Truth;
    You will know mercy and love
        in abundance.
Then will your transgressions be
        forgiven and redeemed.

Psalm 131

Most gracious Presence, let me not
      be arrogant,
    nor boast of my virtuous deeds;
Let me not seek fame or set my heart
    on the riches of the world.
Help me to calm and quiet my soul,
    like a child quieted at its
      mother's breast;
    like a child that is quieted,
      be so my soul.

I shall hope in You, O Breath
    of my breath,
    from this time forth and
      forevermore.
          Amen.

Psalm 132

Enter into the Silence, into the
    Heart of Truth;
For herein lies the Great Mystery
    where life is ever unfolding;

Herein the Divine Plan is made known,
    the Plan all are invited to serve.
Listen for the music of the Holy Word
    in the resounding Silence of
        the universe.
May balance and harmony be your aim
    as you are drawn into the
        Heart of Love.

Those who follow the way of Love
    with calm and faith-filled
        intent,
Know that all is working toward
        healing and wholeness.
And may the healing power of love
    lift you from the limitations
        of fear and ignorance
        into the arms of freedom.
May the peace of the Spirit bless
        you, and
    lead you on life's journey.
Be not afraid of the Silence, for
    Wisdom's Voice is heard there!

As you follow the Light, you become
        gentle and kind,
    you come to live in the Light.
Children enter the world radiating
        the Spirit—
    learn from them of innocence
        and simplicity;
Learn to co-operate with the
        unseen realms,
    to see beyond the veil.

Wise are those who learn through
        silence;
    learn then to listen well.
For beyond the silence and stillness
        within,
    you will come to know a profound
        and dazzling Silence—
Herein lies the music of the spheres,
    the harmony of creation.
Enter into the Holy Temple of your soul,
    converse with the Beloved in
        sweet communion.
Blessings of the Great Silence be
        with you as
    you help to rebuild the heart of
        the world with love!

Psalm 133

Behold, how good and pleasant
        it is
    when brothers and sisters
        dwell in unity!
It is like vistas seen from
    atop a mountain one has
        climbed . . .
Or like the stillness of a sunset
    after a long day's work.

It is like a shimmering rainbow,
     breaking through a
        summer rain.
When men and women dwell in
     harmony,
     the star of Truth appears!

Psalm 134

Come, bask in the Light of Love,
     all you who would serve
        the Divine Plan!
Lift up your hands to the Holy One,
     singing songs of praise!
Bow down and receive blessing from
        the Giver of Life!
     All praises be to You,
     whose Love created heaven
        and earth!

Psalm 135

Lift up your hearts, all you
    who choose the path of Life!
    Sing songs of praise to
      the Beloved—
To the Holy One, who encompasses
      all creation with Love,
    to You, who enter all open
      hearts!
We raise our voices in praise
      to You;
    we call upon your Holy Name!
For You call us your friends, and
    invite us to commune with
      You by day and through
      the night.

For great are You, closer than
      our very breath.
Through You the world evolves—
    in heaven and on earth,
    in the heights and in the
      depths.
In You and with You do we live
      and have our being,
    You, who send your Spirit to
      dwell in our hearts!

Yes, You are with us in the trials
      and temptations of life;
Your mercy and strength uphold us;
    when fear and injustice

prevail.
You forgive our transgressions,
    our shortcomings and wrongdoings;
You lead us home when we have
        gone astray, when we have
    chosen paths that led to
        darkness.
You have given us a birthright
        of Love,
    a heritage of Truth.

Your Name endures forever,
    your goodness is imprinted
        for all eternity.
For in your mercy, You reclaim
        the people,
    with steadfast patience
        and compassion.

The nations have chosen material
        idols—
    the lure of silver and gold.
With their mouths they utter
        falsely,
    blind to the people's needs;
Their ears are deaf to the
        cries of the poor,
    they breathe greed and
        spit out arrogance.
Awaken, O people of earth!
    Unbind the fetters of stone
        hearts
    that balance, and harmony
        may be restored!

O nations of earth, bless the
                    One Spirit!
          O people of the world,
              gather together in unity!
O children of Light, radiate
                blessings to the universe!
          Surrender yourselves to Love!
Blessed be You, O Beloved,
                    Breath of our breath!
          Praises be to your Holy Name!

Psalm 136

O sing praises to the Beloved,
          whose Love sustains us;
Yes, give thanks to the Heart of
              all hearts,
          whose Love sustains us;
And bow down before the Most High,
          whose Love sustains us!

To You, who spoke and the Word
                came forth,
          Your Love sustains us;
To You, who by understanding
                created the heavens,
          Your Love sustains us;

To You, who spread out the earth
                upon the waters,
        Your Love sustains us;
To You, who set the planets upon
                their course,
        Your Love sustains us;
And the sun to rule over the day,
        Your Love sustains us;
The moon and stars to rule over
                the night,
        Your Love sustains us.

To You, who call us to repentance
                and rebirth,
        Your Love sustains us;
To You who accompany us as
                we face our fears,
        Your Love sustains us.
With a strong arm to uphold us,
        Your Love sustains us.
To You who liberate us to live
                into our birthright,
        Your Love sustains us.
Who sends the Counselor to lead
                us on paths of peace,
        Your Love sustains us.
Who comforts us in times of sorrow
                and loneliness,
        Your Love sustains us.
To You, who give us a hunger
                for prayer,
        Your Love sustains us.
And a thirst for You,
        Your Love sustains us.

To You, who are quick to forgive
      and remember not our sins,
   Your Love sustains us.

To You, who instruct us in
      truth and justice,
   Your Love sustains us.
And in mercy and compassion,
   Your Love sustains us.
To You, who open our hearts to
      the cry of the poor,
   Your Love sustains us.
And call us to radiate your love
      to the world,
   Your Love sustains us.

To You, who remember us when we
      are downtrodden and
        discouraged,
   Your Loves sustains us.
And bring light into the darkness,
   Your Love sustains us.
To You, who are Loving Companion
      Presence,
   Your Love sustains us.

O sing praises to the Beloved,
   whose Love sustains us!

$\mathcal{P}salm$ 137

Plunge into the Ocean of Love,
    where heart meets Heart,
Where sorrows are comforted, and
        wounds are mended.
There, melodies of sadness mingle with
        dolphin songs of joy;
Past fears dissolve in deep harmonic
    tones,
    the future—pure mystery.
For eternal moments lived in total
        surrender
        glide smoothly over troubled
        waters.

Hide not from Love, O friends,
    sink not into the sea of despair,
        the mire of hatred.
Awaken, O my heart, that I drown not
    in fear!
Too long have I sailed where'ere
    the winds have blown!
        Drop anchor!
O, Heart of all hearts, set a
        clear course,
    that I might follow!
Guide me to the Promised Shore!

Psalm 138

I give You thanks, O Blessed One,
            with my whole heart;
      before all the people I sing
            your praise;
I was humbled when I came to see
      that You dwell in me, in the
            Holy Temple of all souls;
      my gratitude knows no bounds!
For You are the Holy one,
      the Breath of our breath.
On the day that I called,
            You answered me;
      the strength of my soul
            You increased.

All the leaders of the earth shall
      one day praise You,
When your Word awakens in
            every heart;
And they shall proclaim the new
            dawn of Light and Love.
Great will be the radiation
      of your Glory!
For even as You are the Most High,
      You are Friend to the lowly;
      the arrogant close their hearts
            to your love and guidance.

Though I walk in the midst of trouble,
      You preserve my life;

You are a very Presence as I face
                my fears and doubts;
        Your strength upholds me.
You guide me as I pray to fulfill
                my purpose on earth;
        You do not forsake those who
                call upon You.
        Your steadfast love and truth
                endures forever.

Psalm 139

O my Beloved, You have searched me
                and known me!
You know when I sit down and
                when I rise up;
        You discern my innermost thoughts.
You find me on the journey and
                guide my steps;
        You know my strengths and
                my weaknesses.
Even before words rise up in prayer,
        Lo, You have already heard
                my heart call.
You encompass me with love where'er
                I go,
        and your strength is my shield.

Such sensitivity is too wonderful
for me;
it is high; boundless gratitude
is my soul's response.

Where could I go from your Spirit?
Or how could I flee from
your Presence?
If I ascend into heaven, You are there!
If I make my bed in darkness,
You are there!
If I soar on the wings of the morning
or dwell in the deepest parts
of the sea,
Even there your hand will lead me,
and your Love will embrace me.
If I say, "Let only darkness cover me,
and the light about me be night,"
Even the darkness is not dark to You,
the night dazzles as with the sun;
the darkness is as light with You.

For You formed my inward being,
You knit me together in my
mother's womb.
I praise You, for You are to be
reverenced and adored.
Your mysteries fill me with wonder!
More than I know myself do You know me;
my essence was not hidden from You,
When I was being formed in secret,
intricately fashioned from the
elements of the earth.
Your eyes beheld my unformed substance;

in your records were written
every one of them,
The days that were numbered for me,
when as yet there was none of them.
How precious to me are your creations,
O Blessed One!
How vast is the sum of them!
Who could count your innumerable
gifts and blessings?
At all times, You are with me.

O that You would vanquish my fears,
Beloved;
O that ignorance and suffering
would depart from me—
All that separates me from true
abandonment,
to surrendering myself into
your Hands!
Yet are these not the very thorns that
focus my thoughts upon You?
Will I always need reminders to
turn my face to You?
I yearn to come to You in love,
to learn of your mercy and wisdom!

Search me, O my Beloved, and know
my heart!
Try me and discern my thoughts!
Help me to face the darkness within me;
enlighten me, that I might
radiate your love and light!

Psalm 140

Deliver me, O Giver of Breath and Life,
     from the fears that beset me;
   help me confront the inner shadows
That hold me in bondage, like a prisoner
     who knows not freedom.
They distract me from all that I yearn
    to be,
     and hinder the awakening of
     hidden gifts
   that I long to share with others.

For I desire to be a channel of peace;
   to reflect the beauty of
    creation!
O, that I might manifest your love
     to all whom I meet,
    and mirror your mercy
    and justice!
Guide me, O Beloved, that I may
     become spiritually mature;
   Love me into new life!

For are we not called to make Love
    conscious in our lives?
  To divinize the earth with
    heavenly splendor?
Reawaken my sense of wonder that
   I may childlike be;
That I might flow in harmony with
    the universe, and
  be a bearer of integrity.

I know that You stand beside those
who suffer, and
You are the Light of those
imprisoned in darkness.
Surely You will guide us into the
new dawn,
that we may live as co-creators
with You!

Psalm 141

I call to You, O Blessed One,
suffuse me with your Love!
Give ear to my prayer when
I call to You!
May my supplication be heard as I
surrender before You,
as I abandon myself into
your Heart!

Set a guard over my mouth,
O Holy One.
Keep watch over the door
of my lips.
May I speak only what is of good
intent, and
not busy myself with rumor

and gossip;
incline my heart to what is
beneficial and holy.

Lead me to words of wisdom and truth,
seeds to be planted in my
heart-soil;
Guide me to times of solitude and silence
that nurture new growth,
so the Word may ripen into
abundant fruit.
Cultivate in me a heart great with
compassion and mercy,
that radiates out to all
your creation.

My inner being yearns for You,
O Beloved,
in You do I find refuge and
strength!
May your Light so shine in me that
others are attracted to your
peace and harmony.
In the company of your friends,
may I, too, walk the pilgrim road
to wholeness and holiness,
O Heart of all hearts!

Psalm 142

I call to You from the depths of
        my being,
      with loud voice, I cry out
        to You!
I pour forth my fears before You,
      I confess the doubts that I
        feel within.
When I am weary and my heart faint,
      You are my Rock!

In the paths where I walk, is it
        not You
      Who knocks at the gate of
        my heart?
And are You not the voice of mercy,
      comforting me in times of
        trouble?
Yes, your Presence washes over me,
      like the ocean lapping the
        shore.

I call to You, O my Beloved;
      for You are my refuge,
      and in my understanding.
Come to me in the silence, drop
      pearls of wisdom into my heart.

Forgive me for every unkind word
        and thought;
Release me from the prison of fear

that I might rejoice and
offer thanksgiving!
Transform my weaknesses into new life,
that I may be a gift of your love
to all I meet.
Amen.

Psalm 143

O Bringer of Joy, awaken my heart;
pour your love and blessings
through all my being!
Free me from attachments and desire,
that I may become a clear mirror,
reflecting your love to
the world.

For fear has pursued me, it has
crushed my spirit to
the ground;
it has veiled your light so
that I dwell in darkness.
Therefore, I cry out to You,
O Great Awakener;
Help me to rise once again
like the phoenix of old!

I recall days gone by; I meditate
  on all that You have done;
    I muse on the Covenant of
      your love.
I open my heart to You;
    my soul thirsts for You like
      a parched land.

Strength comes with pureness of heart.
    Cleanse me anew, O Gentle Healer.
This yearning within my soul is
    naught but the inner birthright
      to know and live in You.
Let me hear your Voice within the Silence,
    for in You I put my trust.
Teach me ways of loving service,
    that I might co-operate with You,
      O my Beloved.

Help me to face my fears,
    O Divine Nurturer!
  I call on You for healing!
Instruct me in your Divine Precepts,
    cultivate my soul!
Lead me into deep silence and
      solitude,
    let peace become my mantle.

Divine Light shines in those
    whose lives reflect love.
  As the river makes its way to
    the ocean,
    may I surrender to the flow
      of new life!

Then will I trust that all is
    working together toward the
        wholeness of humanity.
    Then will I help to rebuild the
        soul of the world with Love!

Psalm 144

Blessed are You, O Radiant One,
    You, who are hidden within
        our hearts,
            even as we are hidden within
                your Heart!
You invite us to participate in
    the Divine Unfoldment,
As we awaken from our long sleep
    and give birth to creativity.

Open us that we might recognize the
            divine in every person,
        and become sensitive to all we
            meet along the path.
For You are the Breathing Life of all,
        the infinite and eternal within
            our hearts.

Evoke the Child in our souls,
    that purity and grace might
        flourish!

Inflame us with compassion so
        we nurture ourselves and others
                with healing and forgiveness!
Empower us with wisdom and knowledge,
        that we might bring forth
                the Divine Plan!
And let us recognize the truth
        that clear vision might unfold.

Let us sing a new song to You,
                O Beloved;
        with drums and flutes let us
                express our joy!
You who are Divine Love, receive
                our devotion,
        that we may walk in beauty.
May our heart's ears heed well
        the Divine Word written on
                every heart,
        that integrity and justice may
                dwell within us.

Let each one be receptive to the
                Spirit that inspires,
        allowing the will to respond
                with action;
And may all judgments and denials
                be released,
        that our souls are freed to
                to serve the Light with joy!
Thus will we recognize oneness with
        The Divine Spark dwelling
                within our hearts,
        fanning it to illuminate the way.

Gratitude and inner peace will abide in
                every tranquil soul,
        blessing the universe that
                lovingly cares for us.

Psalm 145

My souls yearns for You,
                Eternal Flame of Love,
        longing to reconnect to
                the Great Mystery!
Every day I will bless You as
        I follow the Voice of truth.
Great are You, who call us to
                childlike wonder,
        to the healing balm of forgiveness.

Each generation must learn anew
                the efficacy of silence,
        the wisdom of turning inward,
That your Light might be their
                guide to holiness,
        and your Love nurture them
                toward wholeness.
Yet, many there are who turn from
                You in fear,
        denying their birthright.

Their denials will lead them further
            into alienation;
        loneliness will companion them.

The Beloved is gracious and merciful,
        allowing every soul free will
            with abiding love.
Gratitude and quiet joy overflow
        as I recall the abundant
            blessings of your grace!

Lift up your hearts, all you
        who choose the path of life!
            My heart is lifted up!
"Do you not know that your whole
            being is
        encompassed by my love?
I am the infinite and the eternal
            within your soul;
        O, that I might make Myself
            known to you!
Choose Love that you might overcome
        oppression and blind obedience
            to false idols!"

"Divine Light shines in those
        who live in Love.
I shall uphold all who are
            burdened with fear,
        and raise up all who call to Me.
The time is nigh for you to choose,
        for great is the new dawn
            that fast approaches;
I call each of you to open your

inner ears, to
see with spiritual eyes,
And to trust that even amidst the
outward chaos,
all is working toward the
wholeness of humanity."

O, Heart of my heart, envelop me!
I know You are near to all
who call upon You.
Bring to my recollection all that
I have denied,
that I might be accepting
and free
To help rebuild the soul of the world
with radical trust, love,
and wonder!

When I speak, let it be of
blessing and gratitude;
let your glory within me shine
out to the world!

Psalm 146

Praise be to You!
Praise the Beloved, O my soul!
I will praise You with all
         my being;
I will sing joyfully and with
         thanksgiving
     to You, Heart of my heart!

Put not your trust in riches,
     in illusionary things that
         fade away.
For when our day comes to depart
         this world,
     at that very time, we carry
         only the love
         imprinted upon our soul.

Blessed are those whose strength is
         in the Beloved,
     whose trust is in You,
         O Divine Lover,
Who gave birth to the universe—
     the heavens, earth, and sea—
         and all that is within them;
Who is ever-faithful, bringing
         balance and harmony to earth,
     nourishment to body and soul.

You free us from the bonds
         of fear;
     You give insight to those
         who would see.

You lift up the faint-hearted,
     giving succor to those who weep.
You watch over those on journey,
     sending guides and angels
          to lead the way;
O, that we might become beacons
          of light
     to those in darkness.

May You, who live forever in
          our hearts,
     loose the fetters of fear
          that bind us,
That we might praise You always
     with free and joyful song!
          May it be so!

Psalm 147

Praise the Beloved, Heart of all hearts!
We are blessed as we sing praises
          to the Beloved;
For as we give ourselves in love,
     so we receive love.
The Beloved abides in our heart,
     in every open heart that
          welcomes Love.

Through Love we are sent to the
          brokenhearted,
     a mutual balm to the soul.
We seek out the downtrodden,
          those without shelter or food,
          recognizing our own poverty
               with them.
Those in prison also await willing
               hearts to visit them,
          that forgiveness might free
               all from bondage.

Sing to the Beloved with thanksgiving;
          mingle with the melodies
               of the spheres!
Awaken to your inheritance in all
               the universe!
          For you belong to heaven,
               to the stars and galaxies.
You come also from the earth, from
               mineral and plant,
          pure water courses through your veins.
Every creature—those that swim and fly
               and walk on land—
          knows you as of old;
And each human—in body or in spirit—
          welcomes you in the heart-song
               of Love,
          where we are One Being.

Praise the Beloved, Life of all life!
          Invite Love into your heart!
For Divine Love gives strength to
               the weak,
          courage to face their fears.

Divine Love brings peace to the
    heart, peace
that is beyond our knowledge.
Divine Love cuts through the ignorance
    that fosters greed and arrogance,
    humbling and breaking open
        the heart.
Divine Love severs the veil that
    separates realms of the
        profane and sacred;
Holiness radiates through all
    touched by Divine Love,
        a refining Fire!
Wisdom flows from the Heart
        of Divine Love
    to all receptive hearts nurtured
        in the Silence.
Yes, the Divine Word is written
    on every heart-scroll,
    a guide to pilgrims on the way.
May everyone awaken to Divine Love,
    that peace and integrity and
        assurance
    may be born again in every land.
O my soul, praise the Beloved!

Psalm 148

Praise the Blessed One!
Give praise from the heavens,
    and from all ends of
        the earth!
Give praise all you angels,
    angels of earth and of heaven!

Give praise, sun and moon,
    give praise, all you shining stars!
Give praise, all universes,
    the whole cosmos of creation!

Praise the Blessed One!
    For through Love all was created
And firmly fixed for ever and ever;
    Yes, the pattern of creation
        was established.

Give praise to the Beloved,
        all the earth,
    all that swim in the deep,
And all the winged ones of the air!

Give praise all mountains and hills,
    all trees and all minerals!
Give praise all four-leggeds
    and all that creep on the ground!

Leaders of the nations and all peoples,
        young and old,
Give praise! Unite together in all

your diversity,
that peace and harmony might
flourish on earth!

Let all people praise the Beloved,
who is exalted in heaven and
on earth;
whose glory is above heaven
and earth.

For all are called to be friends,
companions to the true Friend,
giving their lives joyfully as
co-creators and people
of peace!
Praises be to the Blessed One,
the very Breath of our breath,
the very Heart of our heart!

Psalm 149

Praise the Beloved!
Sing a joy-filled song praising
the Blessed One among
the people!
Be glad in the Creator,
rejoice in Love Divine!

Praise the Holy One with dancing,
 with melodies and voice!
For the Beloved dwells within,
 journeying with us through
 all our lives,
Leading us in truth and love.
The humble are adorned with honor;
 the faithful exult in glory,
 singing for joy with
 thankful hearts!
With truth on our tongues,
 with gratitude as our friend,
We are in harmony with the universe,
 as we hold hands with
 all the people.
The chains of oppression are broken,
 the fetters of injustice unbound.
The realm of Peace and Love shall reign!
 Glory abides with those who are
 faith-filled.
Praise the Beloved!
 All people on earth, welcome
 Love's Companioning Presence
 into your hearts!

Psalm 150

Praise the Beloved!
Praises be to You in earth's sanctuary;
    praises be to You in the mighty
        firmament!
Praise the mighty works of Love;
Praise the glory and extol the
    greatness of Love Divine!

Give praise with trumpets;
    give praise with lute and harp!
Give praise with timbrel and dance;
    give praise with strings and reed!
Give praise with booming drums;
    give praise with crashing cymbals!
Let everything that breathes
    praise the Beloved with their lives!
        May it be so now
          and forever!
           Amen.

Half of the profits from these verses will be donated to Friends of Silence, a nonprofit endeavor to facilitate others in reverencing Silence, prayer, and contemplation and to encourage the life-giving empowerment that derives from the Silence. For further information, write to:

FRIENDS OF SILENCE
R.R. 3, Box 436A
Jericho, VT 05465